Iceland Travel Guide

A Complete Guide for All, Including First-Timers to Embark on a Breathtaking Adventure in the Land of Glaciers

James D. Vollmer

Disclaimer ⚠

The information provided in this "Iceland Travel Guide" is accurate to the best of the author's knowledge at the time of publication. However, the author and publisher make no representation or warranty with respect to the accuracy or completeness of the contents of this guidebook and specifically disclaim any implied warranties of merchantability or fitness for a particular purpose. The author and publisher shall have no liability to any person or entity with respect to any loss or damage caused or alleged to be caused directly or indirectly by the information contained in this guidebook.

Table of Contents

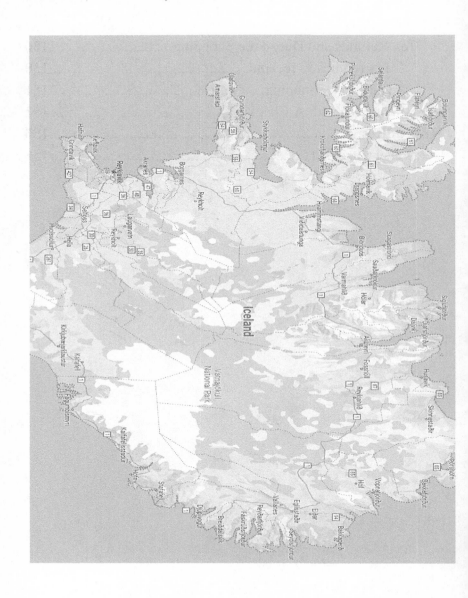

INTRODUCTION

WELCOME TO ICELAND!

My first trip to Iceland was a step into the unexplored—a brand-new adventure in a place of ice and fire that may also present unanticipated problems. This island nation, with its stark scenery, lively culture, and welcoming people, was a location I had long wanted to explore. As I got off the airport, the cold, pure air welcomed me, a dramatic contrast to the busy, packed places I was accustomed to. It was the start of a trip that would not only push me to my limits but also provide me with experiences that would transform my life forever.

Navigating across Iceland seemed like entering a fairytale realm, with each turn revealing breathtaking views. From the dazzling dance of the Northern Lights in a bright winter sky to the deafening sound of waterfalls flowing down old cliffs, Iceland demonstrated nature's raw beauty. Despite its splendor, vacationing in Iceland presents unique problems. Language hurdles, bad weather, and wide, deserted stretches may transform routine travel into perilous expeditions.

One of my first problems was learning to accept Iceland's erratic weather. I rapidly grasped the necessity of being ready for anything. A beautiful morning might quickly become a snowy afternoon. This unpredictability, however, taught me a vital lesson about flexibility and adaptability—not only in travel but in life as well.

Another problem was a sense of solitude amid the huge, open spaces. Iceland's beauty resides in its untamed landscape, yet this may also imply great distances between settlements and the need for self-reliance. I learned to find peace in isolation and to utilize these peaceful periods to ponder and connect more intimately with the world around me.

Perhaps the most difficult hurdle was getting past the initial trepidation of going on such a trek alone. Stepping outside of my comfort zone, coping with unexpected events, and negotiating foreign terrain were all intimidating ideas. However, as I immersed myself in Icelandic culture, met locals and fellow tourists, and tackled each problem head-on, I got more confident and adventurous.

These events taught me important lessons about perseverance, flexibility, and the joys of facing the unknown. They represent the core of what makes travel so enlightening and changing. It is these lessons and experiences that I hope to share with you through this guide.

This guide is more than simply a travel companion; it exemplifies the spirit of adventure and the excitement of exploring the unknown. Iceland has something for everyone, whether you're a solitary traveler seeking solitude and self-discovery, a couple searching for beautiful vistas and comfortable hideaways, a family looking for fun and instructive adventures, or a group of friends embarking on an unforgettable trip.

As you read through these pages, you'll discover insightful insights, practical advice, and itinerary suggestions to help you make the most of your stay in this magnificent nation. From must-see sights and hidden jewels to knowing local traditions and handling logistical problems, this book will help you plan a successful and memorable trip.

So, let this book be the starting step toward your Icelandic journey. Accept the hardships, enjoy the beauty, and allow Iceland to alter you in the same way it did for me. Welcome to the trip of a lifetime. Welcome to Iceland.

HOW TO USE THIS GUIDE

A voyage to Iceland, a region of ethereal beauty and dramatic contrasts, demands not just enthusiasm but also careful planning and advice. This book is intended to serve as a compass, guiding you through the fjords, mountains, and distinctive Icelandic culture, ensuring that your trip is as enriching and smooth as possible.

How to make the best of it

1. Begin with Your Interests: Iceland provides a diverse range of activities, from the peacefulness of its hot springs to the exhilaration of glacier hiking. Begin by determining what attracts you to Iceland. Is it the call of the wild, the draw of the Northern Lights, or the enchantment of its Viking heritage? This guide is designed to help you adapt your travel to your own interests, resulting in a more personalized encounter.

2. Itineraries for All Travelers: Whether you're a lone traveler, a couple on a romantic break, a family on an instructive vacation, or a group of friends looking for adventure, Chapter 9 has well-planned itineraries. These itineraries are designed to make the most of your time and experiences in Iceland, taking into account your duration of stay and specific interests. You can use them as a template, a source of inspiration, or exactly as written—the option is yours.

3. Take a Deep Dive into Icelandic Culture: To properly enjoy Iceland, you must immerse yourself in its culture, customs, and lifestyle. Chapter 6 not only covers these topics, but it also includes etiquette guidelines, words to learn, and cultural subtleties that will enrich your interactions with people and improve your understanding of this unique nation.

4. Navigate Like a Pro: Comprehending the mechanics of travel inside Iceland, from navigating its roads to selecting the best accommodations and comprehending local regulations, is critical. Chapters 3, 4, and 10 provide a thorough review of transportation, lodging alternatives, and legal dos and don'ts, ensuring you are well-prepared and educated.

5. Embrace the Adventure: Iceland's unpredictable weather and harsh landscape are part of its appeal. Chapter 8 focuses on experiences and activities that allow you to experience Iceland's natural beauty in a safe and responsible manner. Whether you want to trek, dive between tectonic plates, or simply relax in a geothermal spa, this section will help you prepare for and enjoy these adventures.

6. Savor the Flavors: No tour is complete without trying the local food. Chapter 5 takes you on a gastronomic tour of Iceland, showcasing must-try meals, dietary guidelines, and the greatest restaurants across the nation. It provides a look into the Icelandic psyche via its cuisine.

7. Plan and prepare: Use Chapter 2 to plan your journey properly. This section covers everything from packing needs for Icelandic weather to budgeting for your trip, ensuring you've covered all bases before embarking on your expedition.

8. Stay Informed and Connected: Chapters 11 and 12 provide practical ideas for remaining connected and safe while traveling. They give information on local communication alternatives, health services, and safety precautions that are essential for a stress-free journey.

9. Reflect and Remember: As your voyage draws to a conclusion, Chapter 13 provides tips for leaving Iceland, from ensuring you have all of your mementos to navigating airport processes. It's about ending your journey on a high note, with memories that last a lifetime.

10. A Closer Look at Iceland's Leadership: For those interested in the geopolitical and cultural leadership that governs Iceland, Chapter 14 offers an intriguing look into the country's president and accomplishments on both local and global levels.

Useful Appendices and Resources: Finally, take advantage of the appendices and resources listed in this handbook. They provide fast references, linguistic aid, and more reading to help you better understand and appreciate Iceland.

This guide will lead you on a voyage of exploration, adventure, and memories. Allow your curiosity to drive you through these pages, and let this guide serve as the road map for realizing your Icelandic dream.

ICELAND AT A GLANCE

Nestled in the North Atlantic, Iceland is a beacon of natural beauty and cultural diversity, where fire and ice combine to create vistas of incomparable splendor. Iceland may appear to be a planet apart, with its huge glaciers, exploding geysers, and mystical Northern Lights coloring the sky. It is, nonetheless, a nation with a rich history and culture, and contemporary life coexists with nature. This section provides an overview of Iceland, covering its geography, climate, people, and distinguishing characteristics that make it a must-see trip.

Geography: Iceland is a geothermal marvel located on the Mid-Atlantic Ridge, where the North American and Eurasian tectonic plates meet. This unusual position is responsible for the volcanic scenery, which includes active volcanoes, hot springs, and geysers. The nation is also home to massive glaciers, craggy fjords, and black sand beaches, providing a broad range of natural beauties in a very small region.

Climate: Iceland has a subarctic climate, with cold summers and warm winters due to the Gulf Stream's moderating impact. However, the weather is famously erratic, ranging from sunlight to snow on the same day. This variety adds to the excitement of visiting Iceland, where being prepared for any weather is part of the experience.

Population and Culture: Despite its wide landscapes, Iceland has a tiny population, with the majority of Icelanders residing in or near the capital, Reykjavik. The country is renowned for its strong feeling of community, rich literary history, and thriving artistic sector. Iceland's culture is heavily impacted by its Norse past, as well as a strong appreciation for the environment.

Language: Since the country's colonization in the ninth century, Icelandic, a North Germanic language, has been the official language. While Icelandic is the predominant language, English is commonly spoken, particularly in tourist regions, making communication easier for visitors.

Economy: The economy of Iceland is varied, with a particular focus on fishing, tourism, and renewable energy. The country is a pioneer in sustainable energy generation, especially through geothermal and hydroelectric electricity, making it one of the cleanest countries on the planet.

Tourism Highlights: Tourism contributes significantly to Iceland's economy, with the country's natural beauty drawing people from all over the world. Key attractions include the Golden Circle, the Blue Lagoon, the Ring Road that encircles the nation, and the chance to see the Northern Lights. Hiking, glacier tours, and whale viewing are all popular adventure tourist activities.

Environmental Stewardship: Iceland is at the forefront of environmental protection, dedicated to conserving its distinctive landscapes and species. Visitors are urged to respect nature, follow standards to reduce environmental effects, and enjoy the country's beauty responsibly.

A Land of Extremes and Beauty: Iceland's attractiveness stems not only from its natural wonders but also from its capacity to inspire awe and reverence for the force of nature. It's a nation where the elements are always at play, resulting in a landscape that is both intimidating and beautiful.

At first glance, Iceland appears to be a contradiction of fire and ice, a country where the ground talks and the sky dances. It's a location that both challenges and entices visitors, pushing them to explore its depths and discover not just the world's beauty, but also the tenacity and warmth of the human spirit that flourishes there.

TRAVELING TO ICELAND IN: WHAT TO EXPECT

When you choose Iceland as your 2024 adventure destination, you are going on a journey to one of the most stunning and unique places on earth. Iceland is a country that flawlessly integrates historic landscapes with cutting-edge culture and technology. Here's what to anticipate when visiting Iceland in 2024, from the convenience of new travel rules to the eternal fascination of its natural and cultural treasures.

1. Advanced Sustainability Efforts: Iceland is a global leader in sustainability and environmental protection. By 2024, you may expect even more imaginative attempts to maintain the land's pure environment. Expect eco-friendly initiatives at every turn, from renewable energy-powered hotels to excursions and activities with a low environmental impact. Participating in these activities not only enriches your trip experience but also helps to preserve Iceland's natural beauty for future generations.

2. Digital Integration in Travel: Iceland has adopted digital technologies to improve the travel experience. Prepare for a seamless integration of technology into your journey, from contactless payments and digital reservations to applications that give real-time weather, road conditions, and natural phenomena such as the Northern Lights. This digital ease allows you to enjoy your journey rather than worrying about practicalities.

3. Improved Infrastructure: With tourism being such an important component of Iceland's economy, the infrastructure to assist tourists is constantly improving. By 2024, expect more accessible transportation choices, such as more domestic flights and eco-friendly buses that connect important destinations. However, the allure of Iceland's wild landscapes remains intact, providing the ideal balance of accessibility and adventure.

4. Cultural and artistic flourish: Iceland's cultural environment is dynamic and ever-changing. In 2024, there will be a variety of festivals, exhibits, and performances that highlight the country's rich creative past and modern inventiveness. From music festivals under the midnight sun to art displays in lava tunnels, the cultural activities available are as diverse as the terrain itself.

5. Culinary Innovations: Icelandic food reflects the country's relationship to nature, with an emphasis on fresh, locally produced ingredients. In recent years, there has been an increase in culinary innovation, with traditional Icelandic recipes being combined with foreign cuisines. Expect to go on a culinary odyssey, from gourmet cuisine at Reykjavik's best restaurants to the simple joy of freshly baked bread from a geothermal bakery.

6. A Commitment to Wellness: The Icelandic practice of using natural hot springs for leisure and wellness is thriving. By 2024, additional health facilities and spas that harness the therapeutic benefits of geothermal waters will have emerged, providing a haven for rejuvenation amidst nature. Whether it's a plunge in the Blue Lagoon or an isolated hot spring in the highlands, health remains central to the Icelandic experience.

7. Respect for Nature: Icelanders have a strong sense of responsibility for their surroundings, and tourists are expected to follow suit. Responsible tourism activities are not just recommended, but necessary. This involves staying on identified routes, respecting wildlife, and following recommendations intended to safeguard fragile ecosystems. Your tour across Iceland is a natural accord in which you leave a small imprint and express your gratitude without limits.

8. Unpredictable Weather: If there is one constant in Iceland, it is the constantly shifting weather. Plan for a variety of weather conditions, maybe all in one day. This unpredictability adds to the thrill, making each day a new experience. Packing layers and waterproof gear ensures that you're prepared for whatever Iceland's weather brings.

Traveling to Iceland, invites you to discover a world where nature reigns supreme, culture flourishes, and sustainability is a way of life. It's an experience that offers not just a stunning environment, but also a stronger connection to the world and a revitalized feeling of awe. As you plan your vacation, keep in mind that Iceland offers more than simply a place; it also provides an experience that will stay with you long after you return home.

PREPARING FOR YOUR TRIP

ESSENTIAL TRAVEL DOCUMENTS

Before embarking on your Icelandic journey, be sure you have all of the appropriate travel paperwork.

What you should prepare:

→ **Passport:** Your passport must be valid for at least six months after your scheduled departure from Iceland. Make sure it contains at least two blank pages for stamping.

→ **2. Visa Requirements:** Many nations' citizens can enter Iceland for up to 90 days as tourists without a visa.

However, this is subject to your nationality and the purpose of your stay. Get the most up-to-date visa requirements and travel advice from the Icelandic Directorate of Immigration or your local Icelandic embassy.

→ **Travel Insurance:** Comprehensive travel insurance that covers medical expenditures, trip cancellations, lost luggage, and other situations is strongly advised. If you want to participate in any adventurous activities, ensure that your policy covers them.

→ **International Driving Permit (IDP):** If you want to hire a car and your driver's license is not in English, you'll need an IDP in addition to your national driver's license.

→ **Health Documents:** Depending on your current health state, you may be required to provide proof of immunization or a negative test for specific diseases. Keep up to date on the newest health standards for Icelandic tourists.

PACKING LIST FOR ICELAND.

Packing for Iceland entails planning for a wide range of activities and weather conditions. Here's a detailed packing list to get you started:

Clothing

☐ Thermal Layers: Base layers that wick moisture are necessary.

☐ Insulating Layers: Wool or fleece mid-layers provide insulation.

☐ Waterproof and windproof jacket: A must-have for protecting against unexpected weather changes.

☐ Waterproof pants are ideal for rainy days and outdoor activities.

☐ Warm hat, gloves, and scarf: Stay warm in colder weather and windy circumstances.

☐ Swimwear for hot springs, pools, and the Blue Lagoon.

☐ Strong Walking or Hiking Boots: Waterproof and comfortable for exploring Iceland's harsh landscape.

☐ Casual wear is appropriate for dining out and touring towns.

Gear and accessories

☐ Daypack: For day travels and carrying necessities.

☐ Sunglasses and sunscreen: The sun may be unexpectedly powerful, especially in the summer.

☐ Reusable Water Bottle: Iceland's tap water is both safe and wonderful.

☐ Iceland's power adapter is European-style with two pins.

☐ Camera and extra batteries: To capture Iceland's breathtaking vistas.

☐ Portable Charger: Charge your electronics on the fly.

Other essentials

☐ Travel Guide and Map: For navigating and uncovering hidden treasures.

☐ Snacks: Especially if you're exploring isolated locations.

☐ First Aid Kit: Put in your medicines and basic first aid supplies. You can check out Dr. Michael Close's First Aid book on Amazon.

☐ Remember that the key to packing for Iceland is adaptability. Layering your clothing helps you to readily adapt to changing temperatures and activities. Finally, make room in your suitcase for souvenirs and Icelandic design things that you may like to bring home.

With the proper preparation, including needed travel papers and a well-planned packing list, you'll be able to fully appreciate Iceland's charm and wonder. This chapter prepares you for a pleasant and exciting voyage, from planning to arriving in the kingdom of fire and ice.

BUDGETING FOR YOUR TRIP

Iceland is well-known for its magnificent scenery and unique cultural experiences, but it is also recognized for its high travel costs. Effective budget planning is essential if you want to appreciate everything Iceland has to offer without breaking the bank.

How to budget for your trip

1. Accommodation: Costs can vary widely depending on the type of accommodation. Expect to pay between $100 and $200 a night for a mid-range hotel or guesthouse, while luxury hotels and remote lodges might cost considerably more. Hostels and camping are more affordable choices.

2. Transportation: If you're hiring a car, consider the rental fee, gas, and insurance. Public transportation and trip packages are available, with fees varying based on distance and destination.

3. Food and Dining: Dining out in Iceland may be costly, with mid-range restaurants charging around $20-40 per person. Grocery stores provide a more affordable option for self-catering, particularly for breakfast and lunch.

4. Activities and Tours: Pricing varies according to the activity. For example, a visit to the Blue Lagoon costs roughly $50, while guided excursions and adventurous activities like as glacier hiking might cost $100 or more.

5. Souvenirs and Miscellaneous: Set aside money for souvenirs, gratuities (not typical, but appreciated for great service), and any other unexpected costs.

How to manage your budget

Prioritize your activities: Determine which experiences are must-dos and budget appropriately.

Book in Advance: Booking excursions, accommodations, and transportation in advance may sometimes save you money.

Consider a travel card. Use a credit or debit card designed for overseas travel to avoid exorbitant transaction costs.

HEALTH AND SAFETY TIPS

Iceland is one of the world's safest nations for tourists, however, it's always a good idea to follow basic health and safety guidelines:

1. Respect the Weather: The weather in Iceland may change quickly. Always check the weather forecast and dress in layers.

2. Geothermal Areas: To avoid burns caused by hot springs or mud pots, follow written warnings and stay on approved trails.

3. Driving: Exercise caution when driving, especially on gravel roads or in winter weather. Always keep an eye out for sheep along the road.

4. Hiking: Tell someone about your hiking intentions, especially if you'll be going somewhere secluded. Always be prepared with the necessary equipment, as well as enough food and drink.

5. Tap Water is Safe: Iceland's tap water is among the world's cleanest. Bring a reusable water bottle to refill and remain hydrated.

6. Emergency Number: The Icelandic emergency number is 112. Download the 112 Iceland app to simply contact us for assistance and provide your location if necessary.

LEARNING BASIC ICELANDIC PHRASES

Below is a guide to some essential Icelandic phrases that will help you navigate your way through this stunning country, from greeting locals to finding your way around.

Greetings and Polite Expressions

Hello: "Halló" (ha-lo)

Goodbye: "Bless" (bleh-s)

Please: "Vinsamlegast" (vin-sam-le-gast)

Thank you: "Takk" (tahk)

Yes: "Já" (yow)

No: "Nei" (nay)

Excuse me / Sorry: "Afsakið" (av-sah-kith)

Good morning: "Góðan daginn" (go-than dai-yin)

Good night: "Góða nótt" (go-tha noht)

Basic Needs

Do you speak English?: "Talarðu ensku?" (ta-lar-thu en-sku)

I don't understand: "Ég skil ekki" (yeg skil ek-ki)

Where is the bathroom?: "Hvar er salernið?" (kvar er sa-ler-nith)

Help!: "Hjálp!" (hyahlp)

I need a doctor: "Ég þarf læknir" (yeg tharf layk-nir)

At the Restaurant/Café

A table for [number], please: "Borð fyrir [number], vinsamlegast" (borth fih-rir [number], vin-sam-le-gast)

I would like...: "Ég myndi vilja..." (yeg min-di vil-ya)

The bill, please: "Reikninginn, vinsamlegast" (rayk-ning-in, vin-sam-le-gast)

Water: "Vatn" (vatn)

Beer: "Bjór" (byohr)

Directions and Travel

Where is...?: "Hvar er...?" (kvar er)

How much is this?: "Hvað kostar þetta?" (kvath koh-star thet-ta)

Left: "Vinstri" (vin-stree)

Right: "Hægri" (hai-gree)

Straight ahead: "Beint áfram" (beynt ow-fram)

Train station: "Lestarstöð" (les-tar-stoth)

Bus station: "Rútustöð" (roo-tu-stoth)

Shopping and Transactions

How much does it cost?: "Hvað kostar þetta?" (kvath koh-star thet-ta)

Can I pay with a card?: "Get ég greitt með korti?" (get yeg gry-t meth kor-ti)

I would like to buy this: "Ég vil kaupa þetta" (yeg vil koy-pa thet-ta)

Emergency and Health

Emergency: "Neyðartilvik" (nay-thar-til-vik)

I need help: "Ég þarf aðstoð" (yeg tharf a-th-stoth)

Where is the nearest hospital?: "Hvar er næsta sjúkrahús?" (kvar er nyes-ta shoo-kra-hoos)

Learning these phrases won't just help you in practical situations; it will also show your respect for Icelandic culture and may open doors to unique experiences and interactions during your stay. Remember, pronunciation can be challenging, but your efforts will be appreciated. Don't be afraid to try, and use every opportunity to practice your Icelandic with locals. Most importantly, enjoy the journey of discovering the linguistic landscape of this fascinating island nation.

TRANSPORTATION IN ICELAND

Iceland, a region of stark beauty and varied landscapes, presents a unique mix of transportation problems and opportunities for visitors. Understanding the choices for getting to and around this island nation is critical for arranging a successful and pleasurable vacation.

GETTING TO ICELAND

By Air: About 50 kilometers southwest of the capital, Reykjavik, lies Keflavík International Airport (KEF), the main entry point to Iceland for visitors from outside. This airport services a variety of airlines that provide direct and connecting flights from Europe, North America, and, increasingly, other worldwide locations. Reykjavik Airport (RKV), located in the city, primarily handles local flights, with limited flights to Greenland and the Faroe Islands.

Airlines: Icelandair, WOW Air (re-emerging), Delta, British Airways, and Lufthansa provide regular flights to Iceland. Budget travelers might hunt for lower fares from low-cost carriers that provide seasonal services.

Connecting Flights: For individuals traveling from locations without direct flights to Iceland, connecting through major European hubs such as London, Copenhagen, and Amsterdam is a popular option.

By sea: Another way to go to Iceland is by ferry. The Smyril Line provides a ferry service linking Seyðisfjörður in East

Iceland to Denmark and the Faroe Islands. This option is especially tempting to individuals who prefer to bring their own vehicle or explore the North Atlantic by water.

To go from Keflavík International Airport to Reykjavik, follow these steps:

By Bus: Flybus and Airport Express provide frequent services between Keflavík Airport and Reykjavik city center, connecting to major hotels and guesthouses. The trek takes around 45 minutes to an hour.

Taxis are accessible outside of the terminal building. While handy, they are more costly than buses.

Car Rentals: Renting a car is a popular choice for those looking to venture outside of Reykjavik. Car rental firms are accessible at the airport and provide a variety of cars suitable for Iceland's many terrains, including 4x4s suggested for F-roads (mountain roads).

Domestic travel: Iceland's internal transportation network is served by air, bus, and, to a lesser extent, ferry.

Domestic flights from Reykjavik Airport connect the capital to significant destinations like as Akureyri, Ísafjörður, and Egilsstaðir. This is a time-saving method of accessing distant sections of the country.

Buses: Iceland's bus system is vast, with lines connecting most major cities and tourist areas. Buses are a dependable and cost-effective mode of transportation, particularly during the summer when services are more frequent.

Ferries link the mainland to some of Iceland's islands, including the Westman Islands, and offer an alternate route to certain inaccessible coastal locations.

Tips for navigating Iceland

Plan Ahead: Weather and seasonal fluctuations can have a considerable impact on transportation alternatives, particularly during the winter, when some routes may be blocked.

Renting a Car: If you decide to hire a car, be sure you're experienced driving in possibly hard conditions. Learn about Iceland's driving regulations, including speed restrictions and off-road rules.

Public transit: is dependable, however timetables might be limited in outlying places. Always check the most recent schedules and consider reserving tickets in advance for longer journeys.

PUBLIC TRANSPORTATION OVERVIEW

Iceland's public transportation network, which is mostly based on buses, provides a convenient method to see the country's cities as well as many of its breathtaking natural sites. While the system is more established and regular in the Reykjavik capital region, long-distance bus routes connect major cities, national parks, and tourist attractions across the country.

Bus Services: Straetó bs. is the primary bus operator in Reykjavik, operating a vast network of routes around the city. Longer distance trips are operated by firms like as Reykjavik Excursions and Sterna, which connect Reykjavik to various places, including the popular Golden Circle and South Coast. In the summer, the frequency of these services rises to suit the increased number of visitors.

Ferries: Apart from buses, ferries provide essential transportation links to Iceland's most isolated regions, including the Westman Islands. This may be a picturesque alternative to road travel, providing unique views of Iceland's jagged coastline.

Public Transportation Tips

Plan ahead: Check schedules ahead of time, especially if you're traveling to or from outlying places with less regular service.

Day Passes: For those staying in Reykjavik, consider getting a day pass that allows for unrestricted transit throughout the city.

Travel Cards: The Reykjavik City Card provides free entrance to public transportation, museums, and hot pools.

RENTING CAR IN ICELAND

Renting a car in Iceland allows you to explore the country's stunning landscapes at your own speed. With a personal vehicle, you are not limited by bus schedules and can visit off-the-beaten-path destinations.

Considerations for Renting A Car

Driving Conditions: Be prepared for Iceland's unpredictable weather and road conditions. During the winter, roads can be slippery and snowy, necessitating cautious driving and, in certain situations, a 4x4 vehicle.

Rental Insurance: Comprehensive coverage is strongly advised owing to the possibility of gravel road damage, sand and ash storms, and other unique driving hazards in Iceland.

F-Roads: If you intend to visit Iceland's highlands, be sure your rental car is equipped and permitted for mountain travel. These roads are only available during the summer and need a four-wheel drive vehicle.

Book in Advance: Booking your rental car ahead of time, especially during high travel seasons, might result in lower pricing and guaranteed availability.

UNIQUE WAYS TO TRAVEL AROUND ICELAND.

Beyond traditional forms of transportation, Iceland provides one-of-a-kind travel experiences that can enhance the memory of your vacation.

Horseback Riding: Ride an Icelandic horse across Iceland's harsh terrain and breathtaking scenery. Horseback riding excursions, known for their pleasant disposition and distinctive tölt stride, provide a traditional and environmentally beneficial method to see the region.

Riding: Iceland's Ring Road and other side roads provide great riding options. Bike rentals and guided trips are offered, catering to both recreational and serious bikers.

Hiking: Traveling on foot is one of the greatest ways to take in Iceland's breathtaking scenery. From peaceful beach walks to strenuous excursions in the mountains, the country's wide route network accommodates all levels of fitness and adventure.

Glacier Tours: For an unforgettable experience, choose a guided glacier trek or ice climbing expedition.

These trips provide an opportunity to safely explore Iceland's beautiful glaciers, including Vatnajökull, Europe's biggest ice cap.

Super Jeep Tours: Super Jeeps, which are designed to tackle rugged terrain and river crossings, provide access to distant sections of the nation that are inaccessible to conventional vehicles. These trips may take you deep into Iceland's wilderness, where you'll see volcanic craters, hot springs, and ice caves.

ACCOMMODATION

Finding the ideal location to stay is an important aspect of planning your Iceland journey. The nation has a broad choice of housing alternatives to suit every style and budget, from luxurious hotels and warm guesthouses to wild camping. Here's a guide to help you find the ideal base for your Icelandic adventure.

CHOOSING WHERE TO STAY

1. Consider Your Itinerary: Before you reserve your lodging, make a list of the sites you want to see. Iceland has various diverse areas, each with its own set of attractions. If you want to travel extensively, try staying in diverse areas to save daily commute time. For concentrated investigation, start in a central spot.

2. Consider Your Travel Style: Your lodging should reflect your travel style and comfort preferences. Solo visitors may like the communal environment of hostels, while families may prefer the space and conveniences provided by vacation homes. Couples may seek romance and tranquility in boutique hotels or country guesthouses.

3. Cheap: Iceland can accommodate both luxury and cheap tourists. Luxury hotels and resorts provide high-end facilities and spectacular sites, generally at a premium price. Guesthouses, bed and breakfasts, and budget hotels offer comfortable but more economical accommodations. Camping or staying in hostels provide the best value for money.

4. Facilities and Services: Determine which facilities are essential to you. Do you require free Wi-Fi, breakfast, or on-site parking? Are you looking for lodgings with a kitchen where you can make your own meals? Create a list of must-haves to help you limit your selections.

5. Location: Where you are can have a huge influence on your experience. Staying in or near a town may provide convenience, easy access to stores and restaurants, and an insight into Icelandic culture. Accommodations in more isolated regions, on the other hand, provide solitude and direct access to nature, but food and activity preparation must be meticulous.

6. Booking Channels: Compare costs and possibilities from multiple booking systems, including direct bookings with the property. Reading recent reviews from other travelers might also give useful information about what to expect.

7. Seasonal Considerations: Iceland's high season lasts from June to August, when accommodation rates peak and availability might be limited. It is recommended that you book well in advance during this time.

The shoulder seasons (May and September) provide a fair combination of milder weather and reduced rates, whilst winter visitors may see the Northern Lights but should expect harsher temperatures and shorter days.

8. Sustainability: Iceland is well-known for its dedication to sustainability. Many motels employ geothermal heating, recycle, and encourage environmentally friendly behaviors among their visitors. Choosing such venues can improve your trip experience while reducing your environmental impact.

Iceland offers a variety of accommodation alternatives, including elegant 5-star hotels and budget-friendly options located in popular tourist regions.

Guesthouses and Bed and Breakfasts

Provide a more personal touch, are frequently owned by families, and offer a comfortable and authentic Icelandic experience.

Hostels cater to budget visitors and lone explorers, offering both private and dormitory-style accommodations.

Vacation rentals: Ideal for families or parties looking for extra room and the ability to cook meals, it is accessible around the nation.

Camping: With several campgrounds around Iceland, camping is a low-cost and engaging way to enjoy the Icelandic outdoors.

HOTELS AND RESORTS

Given the enormous number of alternatives and the ever-changing nature of individual hotels and resorts in Iceland, including contact information, pricing, and availability, it is critical to undertake current research to locate the best match for your vacation plans. However, I can give you a basic overview of what to look for while looking for hotels and resorts in Iceland, including some of the important regions where you may discover outstanding places to stay and what to anticipate in terms of facilities and experiences.

Hotels and Resorts in Iceland

Reykjavik

Capital Comfort: Reykjavik, the capital and largest city, has a diverse choice of hotels, from luxury to affordable. Hotels near the city center or along the waterfront offer convenient access to main attractions, restaurants, and nightlife.

Luxury Picks: For those looking for luxury, choose the Canopy by Hilton Reykjavik City Centre or the Reykjavik Konsulat Hotel, Curio Collection by Hilton, all of which have contemporary rooms and provide outstanding service.

Mid-Range Options: Center Hotels and Fosshotel are prominent brands that provide comfortable lodging at moderate rates.

South Iceland

South Iceland is home to some of the country's most well-known natural features, such as the Golden Circle, black sand beaches, and waterfalls. Resorts such as Hotel Ranga and Ion Adventure Hotel provide luxurious rooms, breathtaking vistas, and outdoor activities.

Unique Stays: For something different, check for boutique hotels and eco-lodges that offer a more personal connection to nature, such as the Frost and Fire Hotel.

North Iceland

Akureyri and Beyond: Akureyri, the "Capital of North Iceland," offers a variety of attractive hotels and guesthouses. For a premium retreat, choose the Deplar Farm resort on the Troll Peninsula, which offers a unique experience with adventure activities and spa services.

West Iceland and the Snaefellsnes Peninsula:

Scenic Beauty: The region is noted for its stunning scenery, especially Snaefellsjokull National Park. Hotels such as Hotel Budir provide stunning vistas and a comfortable, romantic ambiance.

Eastern Iceland

East Iceland provides unique lodgings, such as the Fosshotel Eastfjords in Fáskrúðsfjörður, giving a calm getaway with spectacular fjord views.

Highlands

Adventurous Spirits: For those wishing to explore Iceland's rough interior, the alternatives are limited and primitive. The Highland Center Hrauneyjar provides basic lodgings and serves as a gateway to the Highlands' pristine scenery.

GUESTHOUSES AND B&BS

Guesthouses and bed and breakfasts are popular choices for guests looking to experience Icelandic friendliness and culture. These motels provide nice and comfortable rooms, generally with shared amenities, as well as a tasty prepared breakfast. They are often located in attractive regions, near to nature and attractions, and offer warm and personalized service.

There are hundreds of guesthouses and bed and breakfasts around Iceland, ranging from small farm stays to magnificent resorts. They may be found in every location and geography, from the thriving metropolis of Reykjavik to the lonely islands of the Westfjords. Some are open all year, while others are only available during specific seasons.

The rates vary according on location, season, and facilities, but they are often less expensive than hotels.

To book a guesthouse or bed and breakfast in Iceland, utilize internet platforms like Hey Iceland

(https://www.heyiceland.is/accommodation), booking.com, or Airbnb, which allow you to browse available options, compare costs, read reviews, and make bookings. You can also contact the owners directly via phone or email, or go to their websites if they have one. Some guesthouses and bed and breakfasts require a deposit or full payment in advance, but others accept payment upon arrival. You can pay with cash, credit card, or debit card, depending on the policies of the establishment.

Recommended Guesthouses and bed and breakfasts in Iceland

★ **Guesthouse 1x6**: is a distinctive and creative guesthouse in Keflavik, close to the international airport. It has six rooms, each with its own bathroom and a hot tub built of recyclable materials. The guesthouse also has a lawn, a lounge, and a kitchen for guests' use. The proprietors are a local couple who are enthusiastic about art and sustainability.

You may reserve a room on their website-https://www.tripadvisor.com/Hotels-g189952-c2-Iceland-Hotels.html, contact *+354 421 2800*, or send an email to *info@1x6.is.*

★ **Hlid B&B** is a comfortable and family-friendly bed and breakfast in Myvatn, in northern Iceland. It has ten rooms, some with private bathrooms and others with common baths. Breakfast is served in a large dining area that features a fireplace and a view of the lake. The B&B is adjacent to several natural attractions, including the Myvatn Nature Baths, Dimmuborgir lava formations, and the Hverir geothermal region.

You may reserve a hotel online via their website-https://guidetoiceland.is/accommodation/bed-breakfast, contact *+354 464 4219*, or send an email to *hlid@hlid.is.*

★ **Geitaskard** is a quaint and historic bed & breakfast in Blondous, northwest Iceland. It is located in a refurbished farmhouse from 1897. It features four rooms, each with a communal bathroom and antique furnishings. Breakfast is prepared with locally sourced and organic foods, and supper is available upon request. The **B&B** is located on a farm with sheep, horses, and poultry, and visitors may enjoy the countryside and surrounding rivers.

You may reserve a room online via their website, phone *+354 452 4200*, or email *geitaskard@geitaskard.is*.

HOSTELS FOR SOLO TRAVELERS

Hostels are an excellent choice for single travelers looking to meet other like-minded explorers while saving money on accommodation. Iceland has a wide range of hostels to suit all interests and budgets, from modern and fashionable to rustic and comforting. Most hostels have dormitories and private rooms, as well as common spaces, kitchens, and amenities like laundry, Wi-Fi, and lockers. Some hostels plan activities, trips, and events for their guests. Hostels are available in all major towns and cities in Iceland, as well as in rural and distant places.

You may locate them on websites like Hostelworld-https://hostelgeeks.com/best-hostels-in-iceland-backpacking/,

Booking.com, and Airbnb, where you can compare costs, read reviews, and book reservations. You can also contact the hostels directly by phone or email, or go to their websites if they have one. Prices vary based on location, season, and style of accommodation, although they are often less expensive than hotels or guesthouses.

Hostels for solitary travelers in Iceland

Hostel

★ **Kex Hostel** is a modern and stylish hostel located in Iceland's capital, Reykjavik. It is housed in a former biscuit mill and has a cool industrial atmosphere. It has dormitories and private rooms, a bar, a restaurant, a library, a gym, and a heated outdoor terrace. The hostel also offers live music, comedy shows, and cultural activities.

You may reserve a room on their website-https://www.thebrokebackpacker.com/best-hostels-in-reykjavik-iceland/, contact *+354 561 6060* or send an email to *info@kexhostel.is*.

★ **The Freezer Hostel & Culture Center** is a unique and imaginative hostel located in Hellissandur, west Iceland. It is located in a historic fish factory and features a bright and unique design. It features dormitories and private rooms, as well as a bar, a theater, a gallery, and a yoga studio. The hostel also hosts seminars, performances, and festivals.

You may book a room online at [their website], phone *+354 691 9449*, or send an email to *info@thefreezer.is*.

★ **Akureyri**

Akureyri H.I. Hostel is a pleasant and friendly hostel located in Akureyri, Iceland's north. It is situated in a calm residential neighborhood, near to the city center and botanical park. It features dormitories and private rooms, as well as a lounge, kitchen, garden, and BBQ. The hostel also provides bike rentals, laundry services, and tour bookings. You may reserve a room phone +354 462 3657, or send an email to akureyri@hostel.is.

VACATION RENTALS FOR FAMILIES AND GROUPS

Vacation rentals are an excellent choice for families and groups seeking more room, privacy, and comfort in their own home away from home. Iceland offers a diverse choice of holiday rentals to meet various requirements and interests, from tiny cottages to huge villas. Most vacation rentals provide fully equipped kitchens, living rooms, bedrooms, baths, and outside areas, as well as utilities like Wi-Fi, television, heating, and hot tubs. Some vacation rentals have unusual amenities such as fireplaces, saunas, or views of the northern lights.

Vacation rentals are available in all regions and landscapes of Iceland, from the urban and cultural capital of Reykjavik to the wild and natural beauty of the Westfjords.

You may locate them on websites like Vrbo- https://www.vrbo.com/vacation-rentals/family/europe/iceland, https://www.airbnb.com/iceland/stays, where you can browse available options, compare costs, read reviews, and make bookings. You can also contact the owners or hosts directly via phone or email, or go to their websites if they have one. Prices vary based on location, season, size, and quality of the rental, but they are often less expensive than hotels or guesthouses, particularly for bigger parties.

Holiday rentals for families and groups in Iceland

★ **Hvammur** is a lovely and modern holiday house in Hvammstangi, northwest Iceland. It features four bedrooms that can sleep up to ten people, two bathrooms, a kitchen, a dining room, a living room, and a laundry room. The property also has a spacious patio with a hot tub, BBQ, and breathtaking views of the sea and mountains.

You may reserve this property online through their website-https://www.vrbo.com/vacation-rentals/europe/iceland/reykjavik phone +354 897 4419, or email hvammur@hvammur.is.

★ **Bjarteyjarsandur** is a lovely and rustic farm stay in Hvalfjordur, southwest Iceland. It provides a variety of accommodations for up to 12 people, including cottages, cabins, apartments, and rooms. The farm also contains a café, a shop, a playground, and a beach, where guests may go hiking, fishing, kayaking, and on agricultural tours.

You may book this farm stay online at their website, by phone at +354 433 8831, or by email at bjarteyjarsandur@bjarteyjarsandur.is.

★ **Smarahlid** is a pleasant and large holiday home in Fludir, south of Iceland. It can sleep up to 16 people in six bedrooms and includes three bathrooms, a kitchen, a dining area, a living room, and a gaming room. The property also features a huge yard with a hot tub, sauna, trampoline, and a view of the countryside.

You may reserve this home online at their website, phone +354 699 5500, or send an email to smarahlid@smarahlid.is.

CAMPING IN ICELAND

Camping in Iceland provides an excellent opportunity to see the country's natural beauty and diversity. Whether you're traveling in a camper van, a motorhome, a tent, or a glamping pod, you'll find plenty of alternatives to meet your requirements and interests. Camping in Iceland allows you to explore the nation at your leisure, save money on lodging, and experience the freedom and adventure of sleeping beneath the stars.

However, camping in Iceland necessitates considerable planning and preparation, as well as adhering to certain norms and restrictions. You must consider the weather, equipment, amenities, and expenses of camping in Iceland. You should also respect the environment, the landowners, and the other campers. Here are some suggestions and information to help you plan your camping vacation in Iceland.

Where to camp in Iceland

Iceland has approximately 200 approved campgrounds, spread across all regions and landscapes.

You may locate them on websites like Parka-https://guidetoiceland.is/travel-info/camping-in-iceland, CampingCard-https://www.gocampers.is/useful-info/campsites-in-iceland Iceland-

https://www.visiticeland.com/article/camping-in-iceland/, where you can view the services, amenities, and rates of each campground. You may also utilize the [Go Campers] map to find Iceland's top campgrounds, according to its staff. Some of the most popular and attractive campsites in Iceland include

★ **Þakgil Campsite:** This is a picturesque campsite in southern Iceland, surrounded by mountains and valleys. It has a common space within a cave, hiking trails, a playground, and a restaurant. The campground is open from June to September and costs 2000 ISK per person/night.

★ **Svínafell Campsite:** It is located in southeast Iceland, near Skaftafell National Park and Jökulsárlón Glacier Lagoon. The campsite is comfortable and welcoming. It is a spacious building with a kitchen, a dining area, and a fireplace that overlooks the glaciers and mountains. The campground is open year-round and charges 1800 ISK per person per night.

★ **Bjarteyjarsandur Camping:** This is a picturesque and rustic camping in western Iceland, located on a farm with sheep, horses, and chickens. It provides a variety of accommodations, including cottages, cabins, apartments, and rooms, as well as a restaurant, shop, playground, and beach. The campground is available from May through September and costs 1800 ISK per person per night.

How To Camp In Iceland

The Icelandic Camping Association regulates camping in Iceland, establishing standards and restrictions. Some of the major regulations are:

You must stay at an official campground unless you have the landowner's consent or are in a remote location with no campsites within a reasonable distance. Wild camping is not allowed in national parks, nature reserves, or inhabited areas.

You must pay the camping charge at the campsite's reception, using the Parka app, or by putting the money in an envelope at the appropriate location. The usual camping price is 1500 ISK per person per night, however, this might vary according to the campground and season.

You must respect the environment, the amenities, and your fellow campers. You must not trash, create noise, degrade the environment, or disturb wildlife. You must utilize the campsite's restrooms, showers, and trash disposal facilities, or adhere to the leave no-trace rules if you are in a rural region. You must also adhere to fire safety laws and regulations, and never start a fire outside of a specified location.

What to Pack for Camping in Iceland

Camping in Iceland necessitates certain specific equipment and gear, depending on the style of camping and season of trip. Some of the essential items you will require are:

Tent, sleeping bag, sleeping mat, and pillow. You may either bring your own, hire them from a camping equipment rental business, or purchase them in Iceland. You should select a tent that is durable, waterproof, and simple to set up and take down. You should also select a sleeping bag that is warm, comfy, and appropriate for the temperature range you anticipate. You should also carry a sleeping mat to protect your body from the ground and a pillow to support your head and neck.

A stove, pot, pan, kettle, knife, spoon, fork, plate, cup, and water bottle. You may either bring your own, hire them from a camping equipment rental business, or purchase them in Iceland. You should pick a stove that is lightweight, dependable and works with the fuel accessible in Iceland.

To prepare your dinner, bring a pot, a pan, a kettle, and a knife, as well as a spoon, a fork, a plate, a cup, and a water bottle. You should also bring matches or a lighter to light the stove, as well as dish soap and a sponge to clean the dishes.

A torch, a headlamp, a battery pack, and a charger. You may either bring your own, hire them from a camping equipment rental business, or purchase them in Iceland. You should include a torch and a headlamp to illuminate your tent and surroundings at night, especially in the winter when the days are short. You should also carry a power bank and charger to keep your phone and other gadgets charged, as not all campgrounds have power outlets.

A towel, a toiletry bag, and a first aid kit can be brought from home, rented from a camping gear rental company, or purchased in Iceland. You should bring a towel to dry off after utilizing the showers or hot springs, as well as a toiletry bag to hold your personal hygiene supplies like toothbrushes, toothpaste, shampoo, and soap. You should also include a first aid package to handle minor injuries or diseases including cuts, burns, blisters, and headaches.

Clothing, footwear, and accessories that are both warm and waterproof. You may either bring your own, hire them from a camping equipment rental business, or purchase them in Iceland. You should pack warm and waterproof clothes, such as coats, sweaters, pants, socks, and underwear, to protect yourself from the cold, wind, and rain. You should also carry footwear that is comfortable, durable, and appropriate for the terrain, such as hiking boots, sneakers, or sandals. You should also pack hats, gloves, scarves, sunglasses, and other items to protect your head, hands, neck, and eyes.

Camping in Iceland is an incredible experience that will allow you to observe the country from a new perspective and create lasting memories. Following these suggestions and information will allow you to organize your camping vacation in Iceland with simplicity and confidence. Happy camping! ●

ICELANDIC CUISINE

Iceland is a nation of extremes, where harsh and desolate landscapes meet sophisticated and cosmopolitan culture. This is reflected in its cuisine, which mixes traditional and creative elements, local and global, simple and elegant. Icelandic cuisine is focused on fish, lamb, dairy, and bread, with several unusual delicacies such as pickled shark, smoked lamb, and skyr. In recent years, Icelandic food has become increasingly diversified and inventive, with numerous restaurants serving foreign and fusion meals. This chapter will teach you about some typical Icelandic meals to try, eating etiquette in Iceland, and the finest restaurants for every budget.

TRADITIONAL ICELANDIC FOODS TO TRY

If you wish to enjoy the true flavor of Iceland, try some of the traditional recipes listed below:

Plokkfiskur: This substantial fish stew is cooked with boiling cod or haddock, potatoes, onions, butter, and milk. It is typically served alongside dark rye bread and butter. Plokkfiskur is a popular comfort dish in Iceland, particularly during the winter months. It is available at a variety of restaurants and cafés, or you may prepare it at home using this recipe-https://traveltonorth.com/iceland/what-is-table-etiquette-in-iceland/.

Hangikjöt: This is smoked lamb that is customarily hung over a fire for several weeks. It has a deep, smokey taste and a soft texture. Hangikjöt is frequently served during Christmas, together with red cabbage, potatoes, green peas, and gravy. It may also be found on sandwiches, salads, and pizzas. You may purchase it in stores or try it at Old Iceland-https://www.frommers.com/destinations/iceland/planning-a-trip/tips-on-dining, a restaurant that specializes on traditional Icelandic cuisine.

Harðfiskur: Dried fish prepared from cod, haddock, or catfish. It is a protein-rich snack that may be eaten alone or with butter. Harðfiskur, a delicacy in Iceland, is commonly presented as a gift. It may be found at supermarkets, petrol stations, and souvenir shops. You may also taste it at Fish and Chips Vagninn-https://www.nextexpat.com/en/icelandic-etiquette-and-culture/, a food truck that offers it alongside chips and sauces.

Hákarl: Fermented shark derived from the Greenland shark or other sleeping sharks. The shark flesh is buried underground for several months before hanging to dry for another several months. The end product is a harsh, ammonia-like meal with an acquired taste. Hákarl is typically served in little chunks with a shot of brennivín, a native schnapps.

Find it at specialist stores or at the Þorramatur buffet-https://theplanetd.com/icelandic-food/, a typical midwinter feast including different cured meats and fish items served with rúgbrauð (thick dark and sweet rye bread) and brennivín (an Icelandic akvavit).

Skyr is a yogurt-like dairy product created with skimmed milk and a specific culture. It is rich and creamy, with a high protein and calcium content. Skyr is served as a breakfast or dessert, along with fruit, granola, or honey. It's also used for baking, smoothies, and ice cream. Skyr is one of Iceland's most popular snacks, available in every grocery store store and café. You may also try it at Glo- https://www.swedishnomad.com/icelandic-food/, a vegetarian restaurant that serves skyr bowls with a variety of toppings.

DINING ETIQUETTE IN ICELAND.

When dining in Iceland, you should respect a few basic norms and conventions. The majority of them are comparable to those in other Western nations, however, there are a few distinctions to be aware of. Here are some recommendations for dining in Iceland:

Arrive on time: Punctuality is vital in Iceland, so make sure you get to the dinner table on time. If you are invited to someone's home, you are expected to bring a little gift, such as flowers, chocolates, or wine.

Before sitting down to dine, properly clean your hands with soap and warm water. You may also be given a towel to dry your hands.

Wait to be seated: In Iceland, it is usual to wait for the host or hostess to seat you. They may also indicate where and with whom you should sit.

Before taking a sip of your drink, say "skál" (pronounced "skowl"), which indicates "cheers". Make eye contact with the person you're toasting with and softly clink your glasses.

Use utensils: Although Icelanders have historically eaten with their hands, utensils are increasingly widely used in Iceland. You should cut and consume your meal with a knife and a fork, then set it on your plate when finished. You should also use a spoon to consume soup or dessert and a napkin to clean your lips.

Finish what's on your plate: In Iceland, finishing what's on your plate is considered courteous and demonstrates respect for the cuisine and the cook. You should also try everything that is presented to you, even if you are unsure what it is or if you will enjoy it. If you are unable to consume something, politely reject it or leave a tiny portion on your plate.

Do not tip: Tipping is not typical in Iceland, as the service charge is already included in the bill. You may, however, round up the amount or leave some change if you are pleased with the service.

BEST RESTAURANTS FOR EVERY BUDGET

If you're searching for a good and enjoyable lunch in Iceland, there are lots of alternatives to suit your budget and interests. Seafood and vegetarian options are available, as well as pizza and burgers. Here are some of the top restaurants for every budget in Iceland:

- **Cheap:** If you're searching for a cheap and quick supper, consider one of the following places:

- **Noodle Station:** This Vietnamese-inspired restaurant provides three options: beef, chicken, or vegetarian noodles with a tasty broth. A big bowl costs 1490 ISK and is filling.

- **Hlöllabátar:** A sandwich store that offers hot and cold subs with different fillings including ham, cheese, tuna, or chicken. A normal sub costs 990 ISK and includes a drink and cookie.

- **Pítan:** A falafel restaurant that offers wraps, salads, and platters with falafel, hummus, and other toppings. A wrap costs 1190 ISK and is quite delicious and fresh.

- Mid-range: If you want a more substantial and diverse supper, you can try some of the following restaurants:

- **Slippbarinn:** A stylish and intimate bar and restaurant serving beverages and cuisine with both local and foreign characteristics. You may sample the seafood of the day, the lamb burger, or the vegetarian curry. A main meal costs around 3000 ISK and is well worth it.

- **Hradlestin:** This Indian restaurant delivers genuine and spicy cuisine like chicken tikka masala, lamb rogan josh, or vegetable korma. You may also order a thali, which is a combination of numerous meals. The main meal costs roughly 2500 ISK and includes rice and naan bread.

- **2Guys:** This is a pizza business that sells thin-crust pizzas made with fresh, high-quality ingredients. There are several topping options available, including pepperoni, mushrooms, and blue cheese. A big pizza costs about 2000 ISK and feeds two people.

- **Splurge:** If you're feeling adventurous and want to treat yourself, consider one of the following places:

- **Moss Restaurant:** This Michelin-starred restaurant is located at the Blue Lagoon and has breathtaking views of the volcanic horizon. It provides superb cuisine with Icelandic and foreign influences, including reindeer, langoustine, and skyr. A five-course meal costs 16,900 ISK and offers an unforgettable experience.

- **Apotek:** This sophisticated and beautiful restaurant, housed in a former pharmacy, serves a combination of Icelandic and European food. It offers meals including grilled beef tenderloin, arctic char, and duck confit. The main dish costs around 5000 ISK and is elegantly presented.

- **Dill:** This Michelin-starred restaurant, nestled in a historic structure, serves a contemporary and imaginative take on Nordic food. It offers meals including smoked fish, lamb tartare, and skyr ice cream. A seven-course meal costs 14,900 ISK and offers a gourmet jouney.

NIGHTLIFE AND CLUBBING IN ICELAND

Iceland's nightlife scene is as unique and vibrant as the country's stunning natural landscapes. Despite its small size, Iceland offers an array of exciting clubs, bars, and entertainment venues where locals and visitors alike gather to unwind, socialize, and dance the night away. Five places you must visit for an unforgettable nightlife experience in Iceland:

- ➢ **Kaffibarinn (Reykjavik):** Located in the heart of Reykjavik's downtown district, Kaffibarinn is a legendary hotspot that has been a fixture in the city's nightlife since the 1990s. This cozy yet lively bar exudes a relaxed atmosphere during the early evening hours, perfect for enjoying a casual drink and mingling with locals. As the night progresses, Kaffibarinn transforms into a bustling nightclub, with DJs spinning a mix of electronic, indie, and alternative tunes until the early hours of the morning.

➢ **Prikid (Reykjavik):** Another iconic venue in Reykjavik, Prikid is renowned for its eclectic decor, friendly ambiance, and diverse crowd. This hip and laid-back bar is a favorite among locals and tourists alike, offering an extensive selection of craft beers, cocktails, and Icelandic specialties. Whether you're looking to enjoy live music performances, engage in stimulating conversations, or simply soak in the vibrant atmosphere, Prikid promises an unforgettable night out in the heart of the Icelandic capital.

➢ **Paloma (Reykjavik):** Situated in an old cinema building in Reykjavik's city center, Paloma is a cutting-edge nightclub that sets the stage for an unforgettable party experience. With its avant-garde design, state-of-the-art sound system, and eclectic lineup of DJs and performers, Paloma attracts a diverse crowd of music lovers and partygoers. Whether you're into electronic beats, hip-hop vibes, or indie anthems, Paloma offers something for everyone, guaranteeing an electrifying night of dancing and revelry.

➤ **Húrra (Reykjavik):** Húrra is a hip and happening nightclub located in downtown Reykjavik, known for its dynamic atmosphere, live music acts, and themed events. This multi-level venue features a spacious dance floor, cozy lounge areas, and a rooftop terrace offering panoramic views of the city skyline. From indie rock concerts and DJ sets to themed parties and cultural events, Húrra promises an immersive nightlife experience that captures the essence of Reykjavik's vibrant arts and music scene.

➤ **Dillon Whiskey Bar (Reykjavik):** If you're in the mood for a more intimate and laid-back nightlife experience, head to Dillon Whiskey Bar in downtown Reykjavik. This cozy and atmospheric bar specializes in an extensive selection of whiskies from around the world, as well as craft beers, cocktails, and fine spirits. With its rustic decor, friendly staff, and relaxed vibe, Dillon Whiskey Bar is the perfect place to unwind after a day of exploring Iceland's natural wonders or to kick off a night of bar-hopping in Reykjavik.

➤ **Skÿ Restaurant & Bar (Reykjavik)**: Perched atop the Icelandair Hotel Reykjavik Marina, Skÿ Restaurant & Bar offers breathtaking views of Reykjavik's picturesque harbor and surrounding cityscape. This stylish rooftop bar combines sleek modern design with cozy Nordic-inspired furnishings, creating a chic and inviting atmosphere for guests to relax and unwind. Whether you're sipping on handcrafted cocktails, sampling delicious Icelandic cuisine, or simply taking in the stunning panoramic views, Skÿ Restaurant & Bar promises a memorable rooftop experience unlike any other in Reykjavik. With its laid-back vibe and unparalleled vistas, Skÿ is the perfect spot to watch the sunset, socialize with friends, or start your evening on a high note.

VEGETARIAN AND VEGAN OPTIONS.

Iceland may not appear to be the most vegetarian or vegan-friendly country, considering its traditional cuisine of fish, lamb, and dairy products. However, in recent years, there has been an increase in both demand and availability for plant-based food alternatives in Iceland, particularly in Reykjavik. Whether you are a hardcore vegan, a vegetarian, or simply interested in trying something new, you will discover a variety of options to meet your hunger and taes.

You can use TripAdvisor to get their prices and locations

Some of the greatest vegetarian and vegan eateries in Reykjavik include:

Mama Reykjavik is a fantastic plant-based restaurant and wellness place in the heart of Reykjavik. It serves a wide range of foods, including burgers, bowls, salads, and wraps, as well as smoothies, juice, and desserts. Mama Reykjavik also offers massages, courses, and yoga lesons.

Garðurinn: A warm and welcoming vegetarian eatery including vegan and gluten-free alternatives for its soups, salads, pies, and desserts. The menu changes daily based on the availability of fresh and organic products. Garðurinn offers literature, art, and jewelry for ale.

Krúska: Serving salads, sandwiches, pizzas, and pasta with vegan and gluten-free alternatives, this is a quaint and contemporary vegetarian restaurant. The meal is fresh, bright, and savory, with ample amounts. Krúska offers online ordering and catering servces.

Salatbarinn: This salad bar serves a range of fresh and healthful products, including greens, cereals, legumes, nuts, seeds, fruits, and dressings. You may make your salad or select from pre-made selections. Salatbarinn serves soups, breads, and swets.

Passion Reykjavik: This is a vegan bakery and café that sells cakes, muffins, cookies, and other sweet delicacies along with coffee, tea, and hot chocolate. The baked items are prepared with organic and natural ingredients and do not include refined sugar, gluten, or soy. Passion Reykjavik also offers personalized cakes and catering options.

EXPERIENCE ICELAND'S CAFÉS AND BAKERIES

Iceland has a significant coffee culture, with several cafés and bakeries in Reykjavik and surrounding cities. These are excellent locations to unwind, chat, and savor a hot beverage and delicious food. You may try classic Icelandic pastries and bread, like kleina, vínarbrauð, and rúgbauð.

Some of the greatest cafés and bakeries in Reykjavik include:

Braud & Co.: This modern and colorful bakery is well-known for its sourdough and cinnamon buns. In addition to pastries like croissants, scones, and donuts, the bakery serves sandwiches and pizzas. You can smell the fresh bread from a distance and see the bakers at work through the windows.

Sandholt: Coffee, tea, and wine are served here along with breakfast, lunch, and supper in a quaint and sophisticated bakery and café. The bakery serves a range of breads, cakes, and pastries, including skyr cake, chocolate cake, and carrot cake. The café also provides fish soup, lamb burgers, and vegetarian curries.

Deig: This stylish and minimalist bakery and café provides bagels, pastries, and coffee. Chocolate sea salt donuts, Parmesan bagel, sourdough bread, and croissants are among the bakery's best-known offerings. The café also serves smoothies, juices, and salads.

Geothermal Bakery: This is a unique and traditional method of making bread in Iceland that makes use of the natural heat from geothermal hot springs. The bread is produced using rye flour, water, sugar, salt, and yeast and then buried for 24 hours. The end product is a rich, thick bread with a little sweet and sour taste. You may sample this bread at Fontana, a geothermal spa that provides a rye bread sensation.

EXPLORING ICELANDIC CULTURE

Iceland, a country steeped in history and culture, provides a tapestry of experiences encompassing its heritage, arts, literature, music, and festivals. This chapter digs into these features, demonstrating how they contribute to Iceland's unique cultural identity.

HISTORY & HERITAGE

Iceland's history begins with the colonization of Norse Vikings in the late ninth century, which is well chronicled in the sagas—prose tales that are among the country's most valuable literary treasures. These sagas, written in the 13th century, not only document the early settlers' exploits and disputes, but they also provide insight into the society institutions, laws, and beliefs of the period.

Iceland's legacy is inextricably linked to its natural surroundings, from Thingvellir National Park, where the world's first parliament, the Althing, was founded in 930 AD, to the surviving turf homes that showcase traditional Icelandic architecture. The country's Viking legacy is honored in museums such as the National Museum of Iceland and the Saga Museum, which provide immersive encounters into the life of Iceland's first settlers.

ARTS AND LITERATURE

Icelandic literature has progressed from epic sagas in the Viking Age to a lively modern scene. Iceland is known as a "nation of storytellers," with Nobel laureate Halldór Laxness and current authors such as Arnaldur Indriðason and Yrsa Sigurðardóttir receiving international fame. The Reykjavik International Literary Festival, which draws writers and readers from all over the world, celebrates the country's literary tradition on an annual basis.

Iceland's visual arts reflect its spectacular landscapes and cultural tales. Icelandic art is both a reflection of its natural beauty and a medium of modern expression, as seen by Reykjavik's dynamic art scene, which includes galleries such as the Reykjavik Art Museum and the Living Art Museum, as well as the city's outdoor sculptures and murals.

MUSIC AND FESTIVALS

Traditional Icelandic music includes distinguishing components such as the langspil and þorláksflauta. Iceland is well-known for its influence on modern music, with bands like Sigur Rós and singers like Björk and Ásgeir Trausti fusing traditional and contemporary sounds.

Iceland offers a number of music and cultural events throughout the year, which attract both residents and tourists. The Iceland Airwaves music festival in Reykjavik features the greatest of Icelandic music as well as worldwide bands, and the Secret Solstice Festival provides a one-of-a-kind experience under the midnight sun. Þjóðhátíð, a cultural event held in the Westman Islands, showcases traditional Icelandic music, dancing, and cuisine, providing insight into the country's cultural traditions.

ICELANDIC TRADITIONS AND CUSTOMS.

Icelandic traditions and rituals are firmly ingrained in the country's history, representing a combination of Norse mythology, Christian beliefs, and the tenacity of a people who have adapted to the harsh yet breathtaking natural environment of their island home.

Þorrablót: This mid-winter feast honors the old Norse gods and celebrates Icelandic ancestry. The Þorrablót celebrations, which begin the first Friday following January 19th, feature traditional Icelandic food, music, and dance. The dishes provided are typically acquired tastes, such as hákarl (fermented shark), svið (sheep's head), and brennivín (a powerful schnapps).

Jónsmessa: A wonderful night in Icelandic tradition, celebrated on June 24th, the feast of St. John the Baptist.

It is thought that around midnight, elves and hidden people become visible, and stones and plants have extraordinary abilities. It's a night to sing, dance, and appreciate Iceland's natural beauty.

Christmas Traditions: Icelandic Christmas is a lovely combination of religious respect and tradition, lasting from December 23rd to January 6th. Iceland has a unique custom known as the Yule Lads, 13 naughty brothers that visit youngsters around the country in the 13 nights leading up to Christmas. Children set their shoes by the window and receive presents or potatoes depending on their conduct. Christmas Eve is a time for family reunions to exchange presents and share tales.

The Icelandic Language: While not a tradition per se, the Icelandic language is an important aspect of the country's cultural legacy. Efforts to conserve the language include using neologisms for new innovations rather than copying terms from other languages, which keeps the language clean and connected to its Old Norse roots.

SHOPPING IN ICELAND: SOUVENIRS AND LOCAL CRAFTS

Shopping in Iceland allows tourists to take home a bit of its rich cultural legacy and natural beauty. Icelandic souvenirs and crafts are more than simply keepsakes; they also benefit local entrepreneurs and the economy.

Wool Products: Iceland is famous for its wool and knitted items, particularly the unique Icelandic sweater, or "lopapeysa," which is noted for its warmth and unusual designs. Woolen hats, scarves, and mittens are popular mementos.

Icelandic Design: Iceland's design sector is thriving, with stores in Reykjavik and elsewhere selling anything from modern furniture and lighting to jewelry and home decor inspired by Icelandic nature.

Local Art: Art galleries and craft markets are excellent places to find one-of-a-kind products from Icelandic artisans. Whether it's a landscape painting, a sculpture, or handcrafted ceramics, purchasing local art benefits the artists while also bringing a bit of Iceland's beauty into your house.

Viking-Inspired Souvenirs: From jewelry and statues of Norse gods and symbols to rune stones, Viking-inspired souvenirs honor Iceland's historical traditions.

Food and drink: Icelandic sea salt, birch syrup, and locally created chocolates are tasty souvenirs of your journey. Icelandic artisan beers, such as Brennivín, offer ideal gifts for people interested in experiencing the country's distinct characteristics.

When shopping in Iceland, seek out the "Handmade in Iceland" badge to confirm that you are purchasing genuine local goods. This not only ensures you're taking home something Icelandic, but it also benefits the local economy and artists devoted to maintaining Icelandic traditions and workmanship.

MUST-VISIT ATTRACTIONS

Iceland is a country with breathtaking natural beauty, a vibrant culture, and a fascinating history. There are several attractions and activities in Iceland, but some are particularly popular and famous. These are the must-see sights you should not miss on your trip to Iceland.

REYKJAVÍK

Reykjavik, Iceland's largest and most lively city, is also the world's northernmost capital. It is the country's cultural, economic, and political hub, as well as an excellent spot to learn about Icelandic culture. Reykjavik boasts many landmarks, museums, restaurants, and entertainment alternatives to choose from, as well as lovely and colorful architecture. Among the features are the Hallgrimskirkja cathedral, the Harpa performance venue, the Perlan Museum, and the Sun Voyager sculpture. You can also witness whales, puffins, and the northern lights from the city. Reykjavik is a walking city, but you may easily get around on public transportation or by renting a vehicle. Reykjavik has a wide range of lodging options, including hotels, hostels, flats, and guesthouses. Reykjavik is also an excellent starting point for seeing the rest of the nation, thanks to its proximity to the airport and several picturesque roads. For more information, visit this site https://www.iceland.org/reykjavik/

THE GOLDEN CIRCLE

The Golden Circle is Iceland's most popular and well-known tourist route. It includes three of the country's most remarkable natural attractions: Thingvellir National Park, Geysir Geothermal Area, and Gullfoss Waterfall. Thingvellir is a UNESCO World Heritage location that includes the rift between the North American and Eurasian tectonic plates, as well as the location of Iceland's first parliament. Geysir is home to both the old geyser and the present Strokkur, which erupts every few minutes. Gullfoss is a magnificent waterfall that cascades into a steep canyon, providing an unforgettable sight and sound. The Golden Circle is a reasonably short and straightforward path that may be completed in one day or less. You may drive alone or take a guided trip, and you can include other sites and activities along the road, such as the Kerid Crater Lake, the Secret Lagoon, or the Fridheimar tomato farm.

For more information, visit this site https://activityiceland.is/the-golden-circle-of-iceland-guide-and-map/

BLUE LAGOON AND GEOTHERMAL SPA

The Blue Lagoon is one of Iceland's most famous and popular geothermal spas. It is situated on a lava field at Grindavik, on the Reykjanes Peninsula, near the airport. The Blue Lagoon is a man-made lagoon filled with mineral-rich saltwater heated by geothermal energy. The water is milky blue in appearance and has a calming temperature of around 38°C (100°F). The water is also said to have medicinal powers, particularly for skin ailments. Massages, saunas, steam rooms, and a silica mud mask are among the services and amenities available at the Blue Lagoon. You may also get a drink or a snack in the bar or café, or dine in style at the Lava Restaurant. The Blue Lagoon is available all year and requires advance ticket booking. Blue Lagoon Iceland: Discovering This One-of-a-Kind Wonder contains further information and recommendations. The Blue Lagoon isn't the only geothermal spa in Iceland. There are also additional locations where you may relax and enjoy natural hot springs, including the Secret Lagoon, Myvatn Nature Baths, Fontana Spa, and Sky Lagoon. The Top 10 Geothermal Spas in Iceland has further information and advice.

For more information, visit this site https://www.iceland.org/hot-spring/blue-lagoon/

NATIONAL PARKS AND NATURAL WONDERS

Iceland is a nation rich in natural beauty, with a plethora of spectacular landscapes to explore. The volcanic landscape, erupting geysers, hot springs, and towering cliff faces and ravines are all breathtaking, and the unending diversity of natural treasures will never cease to astonish any fortunate visitor to this awe-inspiring and ancient island. Iceland boasts three national parks: Snaefellsjökull, Vatnajökull, and Þingvellir, as well as other natural reserves and protected areas. These are the areas where you may enjoy Iceland's natural beauty and wildlife while also learning about its history and culture. The following are some of Iceland's most stunning natural marvels and national parks:

Snæfellsjökull National Park

This Park encompasses the westernmost point of the Snæfellsnes Peninsula and is the only one in Iceland that reaches the shore. The park is named after the Snæfellsjökull glacier, a dormant volcano that was the scene of Jules Verne's classic Journey to the Center of the Earth. The park has a variety of landforms, including lava fields, craters, caves, cliffs, and beaches. There is also a diverse range of vegetation and animals, including arctic foxes, seals, seagulls, and whales. The park has several attractions, including Dritvík Cove, Lóndrangar Rocks, Djúpalónssandur Beach, and Arnarstapi Village. You may explore the park by hiking, driving, or taking a guided tour. Accommodation options include camping at the Ólafsvík Campsite or staying at neighboring hotels or guesthouses.

Visit the Snæfellsjökull National Park website https://guidetoiceland.is/nature-info/national-parks-in-iceland

Vatnajökull National Park

Vatnajökull National Park is the biggest national park in Iceland and Europe, occupying over 14% of the country's landmass. It includes the Vatnajökull glacier, Europe's biggest ice cap, as well as several other glaciers, volcanoes, mountains, rivers, and lakes. The park is organized into four zones, each with its own unique features and attractions. The regions are the North, South, East, and West. The park's features include the

Jökulsárlón Glacier Lagoon, Svartifoss Waterfall, Skaftafell Visitor Center, Askja Caldera, and Dettifoss Waterfall. The park offers a variety of activities, including hiking, ice climbing, glacier trekking, snowmobiling, and boat trips. You may also tent in specified areas or stay at one of the neighboring hotels or guesthouses. More information and recommendations about Vatnajökull National Park may be found here https://www.touropia.com/national-parks-in-iceland/

Þingvellir

Þingvellir National Park, Iceland's oldest and most historic national park, is also a UNESCO World Heritage Site. It is located in the southwest of the nation, on the beaches of Þingvallavatn Lake. The park is the location of Iceland's first parliament, which was created in 930 AD and convened there until 1798. The park is also a geological wonder since it is located on the rift between the North American and Eurasian tectonic plates, which are gradually sliding apart. The fractures and fissures that crisscross the area provide proof of this. The park's features include the Alþingi (Law Rock), Öxarárfoss Waterfall, Silfra Fissure, and Lögberg (Rock of Law). You may explore the park by strolling, cycling, or taking a guided tour.

You may stay in neighboring hotels or guesthouses, or tent at the Þingvellir Campsite.

MUSEUMS AND HISTORICAL SITES

Iceland has a rich and intriguing history, culture, and art, all of which may be explored and learned about at the country's numerous museums and historic monuments. Whether you are interested in the Viking Age, the Icelandic Sagas, natural marvels, or recent advances, you will find something to fit your interests and preferences.

The National Museum of Iceland is Iceland's primary museum, located in Reykjavik, and it highlights the country's history and culture from settlement to the present. The museum offers a permanent exhibition of diverse objects, including weapons, tools, clothes, jewelry, and manuscripts, as well as interactive and multimedia elements. The museum frequently hosts temporary exhibitions on various subjects at various times. The museum is open daily from 10:00 to 17:00, with an entry cost of 2000 ISK for adults, 1000 ISK for students and elders, and free for children under 18. For an extra cost, you may participate in a guided tour or use an audio guide.

The Settlement Exhibition is a one-of-a-kind and creative museum in Reykjavik, housed in the Hotel Reykjavik Centrum. The museum houses the remnants of a Viking Age longhouse found during an archaeological dig in 2001. The longhouse, which dates back to the 10th century, is one of Iceland's oldest constructions. The museum employs cutting-edge technology and multimedia to recreate the lives and environments of the early settlers. The museum is open daily from 09:00 to 18:00, with an entry cost of 1650 ISK for adults, 825 ISK for students and seniors, and free for children under 18. For an extra cost, you may participate in a guided tour or use an audio guide.

Arbaer Open Air Museum: This attractive and genuine museum is located on Reykjavik's outskirts. The museum has a variety of historical structures that have been transferred from various regions of the country and restored to its original look. Turf homes, farmhouses, workshops, churches, and schools symbolize many times and parts of Icelandic history and culture. The museum also features a farm with animals including horses, cows, lambs, and chickens. The museum is open daily from 10:00 to 17:00 in the summer, 13:00 to 17:00 on weekdays, and 11:00 to 16:00 on weekends in the winter. Admission is 1700

ISK for adults, 850 ISK for students and elders, and free for children under 18. For an extra cost, you may participate in a guided tour or use an audio guide.

Skogar Museum: This is a comprehensive and intriguing museum located in Skogar, on Iceland's south coast. The museum is divided into three sections: the Folk Museum, the Open Air Museum, and the Transportation Museum. The Folk Museum showcases a variety of materials and artifacts relating to Icelandic people's daily lives, culture, and history, including tools, clothes, furniture, and art. The Open-Air Museum is made up of multiple ancient structures, including turf cottages, a church, a school, and a fisherman's hut, which demonstrate the various types and functions of Icelandic architecture. The Transport Museum displays numerous vehicles and machinery used in Iceland, including automobiles, motorcycles, bicycles, and aircraft. The museum is open every day from 09:00 to 17:00 in the summer, 10:00 to 17:00 on weekdays, and 11:00 to 16:00 on weekends in the winter. Admission is 2000 ISK for adults, 1000 ISK for students and elders, and free for children under 12. For an extra cost, you may participate in a guided tour or use an audio guide.

OFF-THE-BEATEN-PATH DESTINATIONS

Iceland is a nation rich in natural beauty, with a plethora of spectacular landscapes to explore. While many travelers go to major sights like the Golden Circle, the South Coast, and the Blue Lagoon, there are plenty of hidden gems and secret spots to discover. These are the off-the-beaten-path sites that will provide you with a more real and adventurous experience in Iceland, away from the crowds and tourist traps. Here are some of the greatest off-the-beaten-path locations in Iceland:

Trollaskagi Peninsula is a picturesque and mountainous peninsula in northern Iceland, located between the Eyjafjordur and Skagafjordur fjords. The peninsula was named for the trolls that are claimed to live there, and their shapes can be seen in the mountains and rocks. The peninsula features a variety of sceneries, including valleys, glaciers, waterfalls, and beaches. You may also witness a wide variety of species, including whales, seals, birds, and horses. Some of the peninsula's attractions are the Hofsos swimming pool, the Siglufjordur herring museum, and the Holar Cathedral. You may explore the peninsula by driving, hiking, or taking a guided trip. You may also tent or stay at one of the local hotels or guesthouses. You may get additional information and recommendations about the Trollaskagi Peninsula here: Trollaskagi Peninsula.

Berserkjahraun is a huge and mysterious lava field in western Iceland, near the Snaefellsnes Peninsula. The lava field was generated by an eruption some 4,000 years ago and encompasses around 36 square kilometers. The lava field is called after the berserkers, mythical Norse warriors who raged in combat. According to legend, two berserkers were slaughtered and buried in a lava field by a local farmer who wished to get rid of them. The lava field has a distinct and bizarre scenery, complete with twisted and multicolored lava structures, moss, and wildflowers. There is also a wonderful view of the Snaefellsjokull glacier and the surrounding mountains. You may explore the lava field by driving, hiking, or taking a guided tour. You may also tent or stay at one of the local hotels or guesthouses.

South F208: This tough and rewarding 4WD route in southern Iceland connects to the Landmannalaugar region. The route is only available during the summer and necessitates a high-clearance, well-equipped vehicle, as well as considerable driving ability and experience. The route passes multiple rivers, streams, and difficult terrains, offering some of Iceland's most stunning and diverse landscapes. Along the route, you'll pass across glaciers, volcanoes, mountains, canyons, and geothermal sites. The route also travels through some of Iceland's most lonely and picturesque sites, including the Eldgja Canyon, the Ofaerufoss waterfall, and the Holaskjol hut. You may explore the route by driving, hiking, or taking a guided trip. You may also camp or stay in one of the local huts or guesthouses.

Leirhnjukur: This is a fascinating and active geothermal region in northern Iceland, near the Krafla volcano. The location is part of the Myvatn Lake region, which is famous for its volcanic and geothermal activity. The region consists of a lava field generated by an eruption in the 1980s, which is still steaming and bubbling with hot springs, mud pools, and fumaroles. The location presents a remarkable contrast of hues, with black lava, white steam, and yellow sulfur. You may also see the Viti crater, which is full of blue water. You may explore the region by strolling along established trails or taking a guided tour. You may also tent or stay at one of the local hotels or guesthouses.

More information and recommendations about the Leirhnjukur geothermal region are available here: Leirhnjukur.

Sigoldugljufur is a secret and lovely canyon in southern Iceland, near Landmannalaugar. The canyon is also known as the Valley of Tears because to the countless waterfalls cascading down its cliffs. The canyon is not noted on most maps and can only be reached by a 4WD route that splits off the F208 road. The canyon has a tranquil and enchanting atmosphere, with green moss, multicolored rocks, and clear lakes. You can also see Hattafell Mountain and the Sigoldulon Reservoir. You may explore the canyon by hiking or on a guided trip. You may also camp or stay in one of the local huts or guesthouses.

ADVENTURES AND ACTIVITIES

Iceland, a country of fire and ice, has an abundance of experiences and activities for all types of travelers. From the craggy mountains to the deep blue sea, the country's natural beauty serves as the perfect background for a variety of exciting events. In this chapter, we'll look at the amazing adventures of hiking and trekking through Iceland's different landscapes, as well as the breathtaking experiences of whale watching and wildlife excursions.

HIKING & TREKKING TOURS

Vatnajökull Glacier Hiking Excursion: This 3.5-hour excursion is highly recommended on Europe's largest glacier, Vatnajökull, which is known for its spectacular ice formations and breathtaking scenery. The trip is well regarded for its skilled instructors and the unique experience of visiting ice caverns. It is appropriate for most tourists with moderate physical fitness levels. For the most up-to-date price and schedule information, contact suppliers such as Guide to Iceland or local tour operators.

Glymur Waterfall Climb: This somewhat tough but rewarding climb leads to Glymur, Iceland's second-highest waterfall. The climb provides amazing views of the waterfall, which drops from 198 meters, as well as the neighboring Hvalfjordur region. It normally takes 2-3 hours and is suitable for individuals with a moderate degree of fitness. The south side of the trek is suggested for the finest vistas and probable rainbow sightings on sunny days.

Snæfellsjökull Glacier Hike: Climbing to the top of Snæfellsjökull glacier offers an incredible experience for those looking for a more strenuous adventure. The climb takes 3-5 hours and provides panoramic views of the terrain, water, and, on clear days, Greenland's east coast. Due to crevasses and other possible hazards, it is suggested that you attempt this trip with a professional guide.

Reykjadalur Geothermal Area: This less demanding climb is ideal for families and people seeking a relaxed day out. The trip to Reykjadalur ("Steam Valley") includes a hot spring river where you may bathe, surrounded by breathtaking volcanic scenery. The trek is around 3 kilometers (1.86 miles) long and provides a relaxing opportunity to see Iceland's geothermal marvels.

WHALE WATCHING AND WILDLIFE TOURS

Iceland's seas are filled with marine life, making it one of the world's top whale-watching destinations. From the majestic humpback whale to the playful minke, seeing these wonderful creatures in their natural environment is an unforgettable experience.

Húsavík: This city is often called the "whale watching capital of Iceland" because it has so many great opportunities to see whales. Húsavík boat cruises visit Skjálfandi Bay, where you may view dolphins and the rare blue whale.

Reykjavík: The nation's capital offers easy-to-access whale-watching excursions that let you enjoy the excitement of seeing whales together with urban exploring. During your tour, you may observe puffins and  other seabirds, as well as whales.

Snæfellsnes Peninsula: During the winter, whale-watching trips are available on the Snæfellsnes Peninsula, which is a great place for travelers to see orcas.

Aside from whales, Iceland's wildlife excursions may present you with a range of other natural animals, such as the Arctic fox, Icelandic horses, and large colonies of puffins that nest along the beaches throughout the summer months.

GLACIER TOURS & ICE CAVING

Iceland has a variety of glacier excursions and ice-caving activities, notably around the Vatnajökull Glacier, Europe's largest glacier, and the Langjökull Glacier, which is notable for its man-made ice tunnel. From September to April, these cruises depart from Reykjavík and last between 13 and 15 hours. The man-made ice tunnel and Northern Lights trip cost roughly $294 USD. For those seeking a variety of activities, package excursions such as Sensational Iceland - South Coast, Glacier Hike & Northern Lights begin at 246 USD, down from 276 USD (Arctic Adventures).

THE NORTHERN LIGHTS: WHEN AND WHERE TO WATCH

Many visitors to Iceland look forward to seeing the Northern Lights, also known as the Aurora Borealis. The best viewing season is from September to April, when the nights are the longest. Guided excursions are strongly suggested to increase your chances of seeing this natural occurrence.

Tours run often throughout the season, and if conditions do not allow for a sighting, most organizations will provide a second chance to view the lights at no additional cost. The Northern Lights may be seen from places like the Blue Lagoon, however, this is greatly dependent on weather and solar activity. Consider a multi-day tour that combines Northern Lights hunting with excursions to other classic Icelandic destinations like the Golden Circle and Jökulsárlón Glacier Lagoon.

WATER SPORTS AND ACTIVITIES

While particular information on water sports was not obtained directly, Iceland's distinctive environments provide a diverse range of water-based activities, from peaceful kayak tours through glacial lagoons to exciting river rafting on glacial rivers. Summer is often the best season for these activities because of the extended daylight hours and warmer temperatures. Those interested in exploring Iceland's waters should book with trustworthy firms that provide all essential equipment and advice to ensure a safe and pleasurable trip.

To get the most up-to-date information, including booking information and costs, go straight to tour companies' websites such as Arctic Adventures, Guide to Iceland, and Nordic Visitor. These platforms give a diverse range of tours to suit a variety of interests, as well as helpful insights from consumer evaluations to help you pick the ideal experience for your Iceland vacation.

TRAVEL ITINERARIES

10-DAY ITINERARY FOR SOLO TRAVELERS

Day 1 and 2: Reykjavik Exploration and Golden Circle.

Day 1: Arrive in Reykjavik

Begin your Icelandic experience in Reykjavik, the world's northernmost capital.

Explore the city's sights, including Hallgrimskirkja Church, Harpa Concert Hall, and the Sun Voyager sculpture.

Enjoy Reykjavik's bustling nightlife.

Day 2: Golden Circle Tour.

Explore the Golden Circle by renting a vehicle or joining a small group excursion.

Explore Þingvellir National Park, Geysir Geothermal Area, and Gullfoss Waterfalls.

Optional: Relax in Fludir's Secret Lagoon.

Day 3 and 4: South Coast Adventure.

Day 3: Waterfalls, Black Sand Beach

Drive down the southern coast.

Visit the Seljalandsfoss and Skogafoss waterfalls.

Explore Reynisfjara's Black Sand Beach and the surrounding settlement of Vik.

Day 4 - Glacier Lagoon and Diamond Beach

Continue to the Jökulsárlón Glacier Lagoon.

Visit Diamond Beach, where icebergs from the lagoon wash up.

Optional: Book a glacier trek or a boat trip of the lagoon.

Day 5 and 6: East Fjords, Myvatn

Day 5: Eastern Fjords

Drive towards the East Fjords, which are famed for their stunning scenery and quaint settlements.

Stop by Djúpivogur and Seydisfjordur.

Day 6 - Lake Myvatn Area

Explore the Lake Myvatn region, which is rich in geological wonders and bird life.

Visit Dimmuborgir, the Myvatn Nature Baths, and Namafjall's geothermal region.

Day 7 and 8: Akureyri, Troll Peninsula

Day 7: Akureyri.

Visit Akureyri, the "capital of North Iceland."

Visit the Akureyri Botanical Garden and explore the town's quaint eateries and museums.

Day 8: Troll Peninsula

Explore the Troll Peninsula, which is famed for its breathtaking mountains and fjords.

Optional activities include whale viewing in Dalvik and sea kayaking.

Day 9: West Iceland and the Snaefellsnes Peninsula

Drive to the Snæfellsnes Peninsula.

Visit Kirkjufell Mountain, Djupalonssandur Beach, and the picturesque village of Stykkishólmur.

Explore the Snæfellsjökull National Park.

Day 10: Return to Reykjavik and depart.

Get back to Reykjavik. If time allows, head to the Blue Lagoon for a peaceful bath before your flight.

Depart from Keflavik International Airport.

10-DAY ITINERARY FOR COUPLES

Day 1 and 2: Reykjavik and the Blue Lagoon.

Day 1: Arrival in Reykjavik

Begin your adventure by discovering Reykjavik's charm. Explore the Hallgrímskirkja church, walk around the ancient harbor, and have a quiet meal at a small restaurant.

Overnight in Reykjavik.

Day 2: Blue Lagoon

Spend the day in the Blue Lagoon, soaking in geothermal waters and receiving spa treatments for two.

Return to Reykjavik in the evening. Consider having a romantic meal at one of Reykjavik's premier restaurants.

Day 3 and 4: Golden Circle and Secret Lagoon.

Day 3: Golden Circle

Rent a vehicle or take a tour around the Golden Circle. Explore Þingvellir National Park, the Gullfoss Waterfall, and the Geysir Geothermal Area.

Stay overnight at a country hotel or guesthouse.

Day 4 - Secret Lagoon

Spend the morning unwinding at the Secret Lagoon, a less crowded alternative to the Blue Lagoon.

Explore neighboring sights like Kerið Crater.

Overnight at the same location or go to the South Coast.

Day 5 and 6: South Coast Adventures.

Day 5: Falls and Vik

Drive down the southern coast. Stop at the Seljalandsfoss and Skogafoss waterfalls.

Visit Reynisfjara's black sand beach, which is located near Vik.

Stay overnight in Vik or nearby.

Day 6: Glacier Lagoon

Continue to the Jökulsárlón Glacier Lagoon. Take a boat cruise through the icebergs.

Visit Diamond Beach, where icebergs from the lagoon wash up.

Overnight in the region or return to Vik.

Day 7 and 8: Snaefellsnes Peninsula.

Day 7: Drive to Snæfellsnes.

Visit the Snæfellsnes Peninsula, noted for its spectacular vistas.

Visit prominent locations such as Kirkjufell Mountain and Arnarstapi Village.

Overnight on the peninsula.

Day 8: Explore Snæfellsnes.

Continue to explore the Snæfellsnes Peninsula. Visit Snæfellsjökull National Park and Djupalonssandur Beach.

Enjoy a lovely sunset from the Lóndrangar rocks.

Overnight on the peninsula.

Day 9: Return to Reykjavik.

Day 9: Leisure Day in Reykjavik.

Return to Reykjavík. Spend the day exploring museums, and art galleries, and shopping for Icelandic goods.

Consider going on a whale watching cruise from the ancient harbour.

Enjoy your final evening in Reykjavik with a romantic dinner.

Day 10: Departure.

Day 10: Farewell to Iceland.

Depending on your flight schedule, you may have a few hours to relax over breakfast or take a final stroll through Reykjavik.

Travel to Keflavík International Airport for your departure.

10-Day Itinerary for Families

Day 1: Arrive in Reykjavik

Explore Laugavegur, the major retail strip, and pay a visit to the Reykjavik Maritime Museum, which features interactive displays.

Stay at a family-friendly hotel or guesthouse in Reykjavik.

Day 2: Reykjavik & Surroundings

Morning: Visit Reykjavik Zoo & Family Park.

Afternoon: Take a whale-watching trip from the Old Harbour.

Evening: Relax in one of Reykjavik's geothermal pools, such as Laugardalslaug.

Day 3: Golden Circle

Activity: Visit Þingvellir National Park, Geysir Geothermal Area, and Gullfoss Waterfall.

Optional: Visit the Secret Lagoon in Flúðir for a family-friendly geothermal dip.

Day 4: South Coast Adventure.

Activity: Visit the Seljalandsfoss and Skogafoss waterfalls. Visit Reynisfjara Black Sand Beach, near Vik.

Stay overnight at Vik or a neighboring rural hotel.

Day 5 - Vatnajökull National Park

Explore Skaftafell and enjoy an easy stroll to the Svartifoss waterfall. If it is acceptable for your age, join a family-friendly glacier hike.

Stay overnight in the vicinity, maybe at the Jökulsárlón Glacier Lagoon.

Day 6: Jökulsárlón Glacier Lagoon.

Activity: A boat excursion of the glacier lagoon to observe icebergs. Visit Diamond Beach.

Remind: Drive back to Vik or remain in Höfn for a change of scenery.

Day 7: Eastern Iceland

Activity: Drive across the East Fjords. Stop for short treks and to visit the fishing communities.

Stay at Egilsstaðir or neighboring villages.

Day 8 - Lake Mývatn Area

Explore the Mývatn Nature Baths, Dimmuborgir, and pseudo-craters.

Stay overnight in Mývatn or Akureyri.

Day 9: Visit Akureyri and see whales at Húsavík

Morning: Explore Akureyri and see the Botanical Garden.

Afternoon: Head to Húsavík for a whale viewing trip.

Stay: Return to Akureyri for the night.

Day 10: Return to Reykjavik.

Drive back to Reykjavík. If time allows, visit the Hraunfossar and Barnafoss waterfalls.

Evening: Have a goodbye meal in Reykjavík.

UNDERSTANDING ICELANDIC

LAWS AND CUSTOMS

Traveling to Iceland provides an expedition into a region of breathtaking natural beauty and distinct cultural customs. To have a respectful and pleasurable stay, you need to be familiar with Icelandic laws and customs, as well as how to respect the country's pure nature and ecology.

LEGAL DOS AND DON'TS:

Dos:

Driving: Stay on the right side of the road. Always wear your seat belts, and children should be in adequate vehicle seats. Follow speed restrictions and avoid driving off-road, which harms the sensitive ecology.

Alcohol Consumption: Iceland's legal drinking age is 20. Alcohol is sold in specialized stores called Vínbúðin, and drinking in public locations is often outlawed.

Safety Regulations: Follow safety precautions and laws, particularly when trekking or visiting natural sights. Icelandic weather may change quickly, so be prepared.

Don'ts:

Off-road driving is strictly forbidden owing to the negative impact on Iceland's fragile natural environments.

Littering: Place rubbish in appropriate containers. Littering is not only impolite, but it may also result in heavy fines.

Disturbing Wildlife: Keep a safe distance from wildlife in their native habitats, particularly puffins, and avoid feeding wild animals.

Camping is only permitted in specified campgrounds. Wild camping is prohibited in several areas of Iceland to protect the ecosystem.

RESPECT FOR NATURE AND THE ENVIRONMENT.

Iceland's landscape is both stunning and vulnerable. The government has enacted several pieces of legislation and recommendations to safeguard its preservation:

Leave No Trace: Always adhere to the Leave No Trace principles. This includes packing what you bring in, sticking to defined pathways, and reducing your environmental effects.

Geothermal sites: When visiting geothermal sites, follow the signposted routes and boardwalks. Going off the trail might be risky owing to the hot earth and boiling mud pots.

Respect Natural Sites: Many of Iceland's natural features are located on private land. Respect geological formations by adhering to local standards, paying any relevant access fees, and refraining from climbing or damaging them.

Drones are popular for photographing Iceland's scenery from above but must be handled carefully.

Do not fly drones near airports, over crowds, or in protected areas without authorization.

TIPPING AND SERVICE CUSTOMS

In Iceland, tipping is not as customary as it is in many other countries, largely because service charges are often included in the prices at restaurants, hotels, and taxis. Here's what you should know:

Restaurants and Cafes: It's not expected to tip, but if you receive exceptional service and wish to show your appreciation, rounding up the bill or leaving an extra 10% is a kind gesture.

Taxis: Tipping taxi drivers is not customary, but again, rounding up to the nearest convenient amount is appreciated if you wish.

Tour Guides: For tour guides, especially on private tours, tipping is more common. If you're pleased with the service, consider tipping around 10% of the tour cost.

PUBLIC BEHAVIOR AND DRESS CODE

Public Behavior

Respect for Nature: Icelanders deeply value their natural environment. Visitors are expected to share this respect by not littering, staying on marked paths, and not disturbing wildlife.

Quiet Demeanor: Public spaces in Iceland are generally calm and quiet. Loud conversations or noises, especially in enclosed spaces like restaurants or public transport, are frowned upon.

Queueing: Respect for personal space and orderly queuing is important in Iceland, as in many Nordic countries.

Dress Code

Casual but Prepared: The dress code in Iceland is generally casual. However, the unpredictable weather means that wearing layers is advisable. Waterproof and windproof outerwear is essential when exploring the outdoors.

Thermal Wear: For those planning to venture into the great outdoors, thermal wear is a must. This includes thermal underwear, woolen socks, and good quality outdoor footwear.

Swimwear: If you plan to visit geothermal pools or public swimming pools, remember to bring swimwear. It's also customary to shower without swimwear in the designated areas before entering the pools.

STAYING CONNECTED

Staying connected while traveling in Iceland is simple owing to the country's outstanding infrastructure for internet and mobile services, dependable postal services, and extensive news and media coverage. Here's a thorough guide on staying connected throughout your trip in Iceland.

INTERNET AND MOBILE SERVICES

Connectivity: Iceland has among the highest internet penetration rates in the world. Wi-Fi is widely offered at hotels, guesthouses, cafés, and public spaces such as libraries and museums. Many buses, particularly those connecting cities, provide free Wi-Fi.

Mobile Services: For individuals who want mobile data, acquiring a local SIM card upon arrival is a practical choice. Siminn, Vodafone, and Nova are the primary service providers, with various packages designed for short-term tourists. These may be obtained at Keflavik Airport, service provider locations, and some convenience stores.

Coverage: Most metropolitan regions and popular tourist destinations are well-served by mobile network coverage. However, distant places, particularly in the highlands, may have minimal or no service.

POSTAL SERVICES

Post Offices: Iceland Post operates across the country, offering local and international mail and parcel delivery services. Post offices are found in all major towns and cities.

Operating hours: Most post offices in Iceland are open Monday through Friday, from 9:00 a.m. to 4:30 p.m. Some establishments, especially in Reykjavik, may provide longer hours or weekend service.

Postcards and Stamps: Travelers often send postcards to share their experiences. Postcards and stamps may be purchased in post offices, tourist stores, and even hotels.

Emergency Contacts:

Emergency Number: 112 is Iceland's universal emergency number. It can be called for any form of emergency, such as medical, fire, or police help. The service is provided 24 hours a day, seven days a week, and operators speak English.

App for Safety: It is recommended that travelers download the 112 Iceland app. It allows you to contact someone for assistance with the touch of a button and provides your position to emergency personnel. The software also has a check-in option, which is important for individuals trekking into rural places.

NEWS AND MEDIA OUTLETS

English Language Resources: Iceland Monitor (icelandmonitor.mbl.is) offers English-language updates on local news, culture, and events. The Reykjavik Grapevine (grapevine.is) is another popular English-language site for news, entertainment, and travel recommendations.

Radio and TV: The national broadcaster, RÚV, provides services for both radio and television in Icelandic. RÚV offers news in English on its website.

Social Media and Applications: For up-to-date information, especially about weather updates, road conditions (Vegagerðin), and aurora forecasts, a lot of locals and tourists utilize social media platforms and applications.

HEALTH AND SAFETY

Iceland is known for its low crime rates, clean environment, and excellent healthcare facilities. Travelers can have a safe trip by following standard safety procedures comparable to those in their own country. Remember that the emergency number in Iceland is 112, which links you to the police, ambulance, and fire departments. It is strongly advised to download the 112 Icelandic emergency app, which allows you to contact for assistance and leave your position with the Icelandic rescue squad (Fun Iceland).

HEALTH CARE AND HOSPITALS

Iceland provides excellent healthcare and emergency services, with hospitals and medical facilities situated in all major towns. Pharmacies, or "Apótek" in Icelandic, are also frequently available. In an emergency, phoning 112 is the quickest method to seek assistance. For less urgent medical treatment, consult general practitioners at health care centers or the after-hours clinic, Laeknavaktin, in Reykjavík (see What's On in Reykjavík).

TRAVEL INSURANCE

It is critical to obtain travel insurance that covers medical emergencies, accidents, theft, and loss. To avoid being charged in full for medical treatments, EU/EEA nationals must have a European Health Insurance Card (EHIC). Non-EU/EEA nationals should confirm that their insurance covers healthcare services in Iceland and that adventure activities such as snowmobiling or hiking are covered (Fun Iceland).

Safety Advice for Rural Areas and Outdoor Activities

Iceland's landscape provides incomparable beauty, but it takes preparation and prudence.

Always check the weather forecast and road conditions, particularly during the winter.

Avoid risky shorelines and never climb on icebergs.

When trekking or visiting distant locations, notify someone of your plans or leave an itinerary with the Icelandic rescue team via the 112 app.

Driving conditions in Iceland might differ greatly from those at home; be sure your car is appropriate for your travel plans, especially if you're going into the highlands or during the winter (Nordic Visitor).

Iceland's commitment to safeguarding its tourists' safety and health, along with a little planning and understanding on the part of travelers, results in a safe and happy stay in this breathtaking nation. Whether you're bathing in geothermal pools, exploring volcanic landscapes, or looking for the Northern Lights, understanding these health and safety recommendations will let you focus on the trip while being safe.

NATURAL HAZARDS AND SAFETY PRECAUTIONS

Volcanoes and geothermal areas: Active volcanic systems characterize Iceland's geology. While volcanoes like as Bardarbunga and Grimsvotn are regularly monitored for signs of instability, visitors should always follow local warnings and limitations, particularly when visiting geothermal zones. The appeal of geysers and hot springs, such as the famed Strokkur, requires caution because the water is scorching and the surfaces can be slippery (World Nomads).

Volcanic Mud and Glacial Outbursts (Jokulhlaups): Eruptions beneath ice caps can cause abrupt floods known as jokulhlaups, which pose a threat to neighboring communities. Lahars, or volcanic mudflows, can also occur, particularly during warm weather or heavy rains. These dangers highlight the significance of being informed via official sources such as the Icelandic Meteorological Office and adhering to any travel restrictions (World Nomads).

Avalanches and Landslides: Certain sections of Iceland are vulnerable to avalanches and landslides, particularly during the winter and in hilly terrain. Travelers considering outdoor activities should verify current conditions and predictions, avoid recognized danger locations, and adhere to local authorities' and the Icelandic Association for Search and Rescue (ICE-SAR) instructions (Safetravel).

Weather Conditions: Iceland's weather may vary quickly, offering problems all year round. Winter is characterized by high winds, snow, and restricted visibility, while summers can be surprisingly chilly and damp. Always dress in layers, bring waterproof and windproof gear, and use the Safetravel website or app to get alerts and submit travel plans for longer trips.

Preparation and Awareness: Being well prepared is essential for having a safe time in Iceland. This involves communicating travel arrangements to ICE-SAR via the Safetravel app, which also allows travelers to get notifications and submit their GPS position in the event of an emergency. Donations to ICE-SAR help to fund volunteer rescue services, which ensure the safety of both locals and tourists (Safetravel).

ICELAND'S PRESIDENT AND

ACHIEVEMENTS

BIOGRAPHY OF THE PRESIDENT

The 6th President of Iceland, Guðni Th. Jóhannesson, has a notable career as a historian and professor before entering office on August 1, 2016. He was re-elected for another four-year term on June 28, 2020. Jóhannesson, born on June 26, 1968, in Reykjavik, has an exceptional educational background that includes a Bachelor of Arts in History and Political Science from Warwick University, an M.A. in History from the University of Iceland, and a Ph.D. in History from Queen Mary University of London. His academic background includes positions as a lecturer and professor at the University of Iceland, Bifröst University, and the University of London. Jóhannesson's study focuses on contemporary Icelandic history, including the Cod Wars, the 2008-11 Icelandic financial crisis, and the Icelandic presidency itself.

Jóhannesson's presidency is notable for its unattached political posture, which seeks to be "less political" while promoting Iceland's unity. He has been a popular personality, with high popularity ratings, and has participated in major national conversations, such as government formation negotiations following the 2016 legislative elections. His personal life has a strong family focus; he is married to Canadian Eliza Jean Reid, with whom he has four children, and he has a daughter from a previous marriage. The pair has lived in Iceland since 2003.

To learn more about President Guðni Th. Jóhannesson's activities, speeches, and the presidential office, visit the official website.

His rise from academics to the presidency demonstrates a strong devotion to Icelandic history and culture, and his term represents a commitment to public service, inclusion, and the well-being of all Icelanders.

ICELAND'S GLOBAL CONTRIBUTIONS

Iceland has made important contributions to global issues such as the environment, sustainable development, and humanitarian endeavors. The country's competence in geothermal energy has positioned it as a pioneer in clean and renewable energy sources, helping not only its residents but also expanding its knowledge and support globally, particularly in East Africa. Iceland has co-financed the African Rift Geothermal Development Facility Project in partnership with the United Nations Environment Programme (UNEP) to encourage geothermal investments in several East African countries, demonstrating its commitment to promoting sustainable energy solutions around the world.

Furthermore, Iceland has underlined its commitment to meeting the Sustainable Development Goals (SDGs) by emphasizing efforts such as improving resource efficiency, lowering urban environmental impact, and incorporating climate change mitigation measures into national policy. The government has actively worked toward carbon neutrality by 2040 and intends to maintain the maritime environment by eliminating marine litter and managing fish populations sustainably (European Environment Agency).

Iceland's approach to international development cooperation is based on ideals that promote human rights, gender equality, and sustainable development. The government has prioritized efforts to eradicate poverty, enhance living conditions, and respect for human rights, with a special emphasis on empowering women and girls, expanding education and health facilities, and strengthening capacity for climate mitigation and adaptation. Iceland's development cooperation strategy for 2024-2028 reflects these themes, demonstrating the country's commitment to promoting good change in partner countries such as Malawi, Sierra Leone, and Uganda (Government of Iceland).

Iceland's worldwide contributions demonstrate its proactive approach to harnessing its strengths in renewable energy, environmental preservation, and fair development to support the global quest for sustainability and resilience. For further information on Iceland's worldwide contributions and international development cooperation, please see the UNEP website, the European Environment Agency website, and the

Government of Iceland's official page on International Development Cooperation.

ACHIEVEMENTS AND RECORDS

Since 2016, Iceland's President, Guðni Th. Jóhannesson, has played a key role in promoting national unity and stability. Throughout his term, he has prioritized inclusion, education, and diplomacy, demonstrating a dedication to both national and international advancement.

Jóhannesson, a historian by profession, has used his extensive knowledge of Iceland's history to address current concerns, emphasizing the need of historical context in crafting policies and cultivating a collective national identity. His friendly nature and candor have greatly contributed to his strong popularity among Icelanders.

Jóhannesson has represented Iceland on a number of international forums, highlighting the country's dedication to sustainable development, renewable energy, and climate change mitigation. His support for gender equality and LGBTQ+ rights is particularly significant, reflecting Iceland's progressive attitude on these subjects.

Jóhannesson's reelection in 2020 demonstrates his accomplishments and the public's confidence in his leadership. Under his leadership, Iceland has strengthened its status as a global leader in human rights, environmental stewardship, and peacekeeping.

DEPARTING ICELAND

To ensure a seamless departure from Iceland, it's important to understand the checkout processes for your accommodation and departure customs at Keflavík International Airport, the country's primary international gateway. Here's a guide to help you go through the procedure smoothly.

CHECKOUT PROCEDURES FOR ACCOMMODATIONS

Know Your Checkout Time: Most lodgings in Iceland have a checkout time between 10:00 AM and 12:00 PM. Make sure you are aware of this time to prevent incurring any further expenses.

Room Inspection: Conduct a final sweep of your room to verify you haven't left any personal belongings behind. Check the cabinets, closets, and bathroom.

Trash Disposal: Make sure you dispose of any rubbish in appropriate containers. Icelanders are quite ecologically sensitive, thus sorting recyclables is welcomed if your accommodation offers this service.

Return keys or key cards to the front desk unless otherwise advised. Some establishments may offer a key drop box for early departures.

Settle Any Outstanding Costs: If you have any further costs (e.g., minibar, room service), be sure you settle them at checkout.

Many establishments enjoy it when you provide comments or complete a leaving survey. This improves services for future guests.

Depart from Keflavík International Airport.

Arrival Time: For international flights, it is advised that you be at the airport at least two hours before your planned departure. Allowing additional time during busy travel periods is advisable since lengthier lineups at check-in and security may occur.

Check-In and Baggage Drop: If you did not check in online, go to your airline's check-in counter. Then, drop off any checked bags in the appropriate location.

Security Screening: Take your devices bigger than a smartphone out of your carry-on for examination, and place your liquids in a transparent, resealable plastic bag to prepare for security screening.

Duty-Free Shopping and VAT Refund: There are several duty-free shopping alternatives available at Keflavík Airport. If you are entitled to a VAT refund on purchases made in Iceland, make sure to complete it before leaving. The VAT refund office is located in the departure's gallery.

Gate Information: Check the airport monitors for your flight's gate and boarding time. Gate locations may be a walk from the main departure lounge, so allow enough time to get there.

Enjoy Airport Amenities: The airport has culinary options, lounges, and free Wi-Fi while you wait for your trip.

TAX REFUNDS AND DUTY-FREE SHOPPING

Tax refunds in Iceland

Travelers in Iceland can claim a VAT (Value-Added Tax) return for products purchased during their trip, as long as they are removed from the country within three months. The VAT rate can drastically lower the price of certain things, making shopping in Iceland more tempting.

Eligibility: You must have a permanent residence outside of Iceland, and the products must exceed 6000 ISK on every sales receipt.

Look for stores with the "Tax-Free Shopping" sign. Request a Tax-Free form at the time of purchase and make sure it is properly completed.

Refund locations: To check in at Keflavík International Airport, bring your completed Tax-Free form, passport, receipts, and purchased products to customs officers for confirmation. Then, head to the refund counter to process your VAT refund.

Duty-free Shopping

Keflavík International Airport has duty-free shopping possibilities. Duty-free shopping is a wonderful method to save money on Icelandic products, alcohol, and tobacco compared to city costs.

Restrictions: Be aware of your home country's customs restrictions about duty-free purchases to prevent any problems while returning.

Selection: Popular duty-free purchases include Icelandic wool products, skincare using native components, and local spirits.

LEAVING ICELAND: A CHECKLIST

Task	Description
Confirm Flight Details	Check your flight status and departure time 24 hours before your scheduled departure.
Packing	Ensure all your belongings are packed, leaving room for any last-minute items or souvenirs.
Accommodation Checkout	Know your checkout time and complete any necessary procedures.
Rental Car Return	If you rented a car, confirm the return location and time with the rental agency.

Tax-Free Forms	Complete and validate your Tax-Free shopping forms before arriving at the airport.
Arrive Early at the Airport	Arrive at least 2-3 hours before your flight to allow time for check-in, security, and any potential delays.
Customs and Duty-Free	Visit customs if you need items validated for a tax refund and make any last-minute duty-free purchases.
Boarding Pass and ID	Have your boarding pass and passport easily accessible for check-in, security, and boarding.

Travel Documents	Ensure you have all necessary travel documents, including visas, insurance information, and itineraries.
Electronic Devices Charged	Charge your electronic devices and carry a power bank if necessary, especially for long flights.
Snacks and Water	Purchase snacks and fill your water bottle after passing through security.

APPENDICES

This section provides a comprehensive checklist for travelers and a curated list of recommended resources for planning and enjoying your trip to Iceland.

TRAVEL CHECKLIST

Task	Description	☐
Passport and Visa	Ensure your passport is valid for at least 6 months after your trip. Check visa requirements.	☐
Travel Insurance	Purchase travel insurance covering health, trip cancellation, and luggage.	☐

Flight Tickets	Confirm flight bookings and check-in online if available.	☐
Accommodation Confirmations	Print or save digital copies of hotel or rental bookings.	☐
Car Rental Reservations	Confirm booking and check required documents (license, credit card).	☐
International Driving Permit	If your license is not in English, obtain an IDP.	☐
Currency Exchange	Obtain Icelandic króna (ISK) for initial expenses.	☐

Credit/Debit Cards	Inform the bank of travel plans. Check for international transaction fees.	☐
Electronic Devices	Charge all devices and pack chargers and adapters.	☐
Medications	Pack prescription medications with original packaging and doctor's note.	☐
First-Aid Kit	Assemble a travel-sized first-aid kit.	☐
Weather-Appropriate Clothing	Pack layers, waterproof and windproof jackets, and sturdy walking shoes.	☐

Snacks and Water Bottle	Bring snacks for long excursions and a reusable water bottle.	☐
Maps and Guidebooks	Download digital maps or print out necessary guides and itineraries.	☐
Language Guide	Learn basic Icelandic phrases or download a language app.	☐
Emergency Contacts	List of emergency contacts, including local embassy and services in Iceland.	☐

Recommended Resources

- Inspired by Iceland - The official tourism website of Iceland, offering comprehensive information on travel, accommodation, and activities.

- SafeTravel.is - Essential for checking road conditions, weather updates, and safety advice.

- Icelandic Meteorological Office - For weather forecasts to plan your daily activities.

- Visit Reykjavik - For insights into the capital's attractions, dining, and events.

- Guide to Iceland - A platform for booking tours, finding accommodations, and reading travel articles.

Have a Memorable Trip

Made in United States
North Haven, CT
17 April 2024

51416752R00096